American Woodworker

HOW TO MAKE
Bookshelves
& Bookcases

19 OUTSTANDING STORAGE PROJECTS
from the Experts at American Woodworker

FOX CHAPEL
PUBLISHING

Published by Fox Chapel Publishing Company, Inc., 1970 Broad St., East Petersburg, PA 17520, 717-560-4703, www.FoxChapelPublishing.com

American Woodworker, ISSN 1074-9152, USPS 738-710, is published bimonthly by Woodworking Media, LLC, 90 Sherman St., Cambridge, MA 02140, www.AmericanWoodworker.com.

Library of Congress Control Number: 2009053479
ISBN-13: 978-1-56523-458-1
ISBN-10: 1-56523-458-8

Library of Congress Cataloging-in-Publication Data

How to make bookshelves & bookcases.

    p. cm.

Includes index.

ISBN 978-1-56523-458-1

1. Bookcases. 2. Shelving (Furniture) I. Fox Chapel Publishing.

TT197.5.B6H66 2010

684.1'6--dc22

                        2009053479

To learn more about the other great books from Fox Chapel Publishing, or to find a retailer near you, call toll-free 800-457-9112 or visit us at *www.FoxChapelPublishing.com*.

Printed in China
First printing: May 2010

HOW TO MAKE
Bookshelves
& Bookcases

Contents

What You Can
Learn and Make

How to defy gravity (Cantlevered Shelves, page 26, and Floating Shelves, page 32)

How to design for large and heavy loads (Stronger Shelves, page 10)

How to defeat dust with glass doors that hinge open (Display Cabinet, page 108, and Grand Bookcase, page 160), and with doors that slide (Sliding Door Bookcase, page 98)

How to knock out some handy little storage in less than a weekend (Swedish Wall Shelf, page 20, Free-Form Shelf, page 75, Cottage Bookcase, page 80)

How to conquer complexity with cases that come apart (Contemporary Bookcase, page 64, and Craftsman Bookcase, page 120)

How to conquer space with sectional cases (Two-Part Bookcase, page 88, and Mantel Bookcase, page 150)

How to design with style to complement your home decor (Slding Bookrack, page 16, Walnut Wall Shelves, page 42, Bow-Front Bookcase, page 52, and Sapele Display Cabinet, page 172)

How to simplify construction with built-in cases (Floor to Ceiling Bookcase, page 140).

Introduction

Whether you live in an apartment, a condominium, or a house, you're going to be faced with the bookshelf problem. That is, what are you going to do with the books you collect, the trophies, and *objets d'art* you acquire, the CDs and DVDs you can't live without, not to mention the toys.

You'll probably visit the furniture store—bah, too darn expensive—and the discount merchandiser—bah, cheesy junk. You're going to end up wanting to make the storage and display shelves you need.

Maybe they can be open shelves. Maybe they need glass doors for dust-free display. Maybe you want to hang shelving on the wall. Maybe you want it to stand on the floor. Maybe it should be built in. But how wide can you make a shelf before it sags under load? How deep does it have to be to house electronic equipment? How tall before you can't get it out of the workshop? Plywood? Solid wood? There are many decisions, but fortunately, help is at hand in this book of shop-tested bookshelf and bookcase projects from American Woodworker magazine.

These projects feature detailed shop drawings with complete bills of materials, along with step-by-step instructions. Sharp photos show you exactly what the results should look like. You're never left guessing which part goes where, and which step to take next.

So, here's to fun and success in the workshop, plus the satisfaction of knowing you've made something really nice to grace your family's home.

Randy Johnson,

Editorial Director, *American Woodworker* magazine

Bow-Front Bookcase,
page 52

by TOM CASPAR

Stronger Shelves

DESIGNING SAG-PROOF SHELVES

Have you ever heard a shelf groan? Well, maybe not, but some shelves look as if they would if they could. So much stuff gets piled on them that they end up sagging like a limp noodle. It's not a pretty sight. A span that holds up weight should look strong and sturdy. Even a slight sag sends an unappealing visual message.

A shelf sags in two stages. There's a small sag when you first put weight on the shelf. This sag, or deflection, increases as more stuff is loaded on the shelf over the years. The shelf keeps on sagging, a little more each year, because wood slowly but surely changes shape under a load. This characteristic of wood is called "creep."

Figure A: The ABCs of Holding Up Weight

Changing any dimension affects the rigidity of a shelf. The biggest returns come with adding thickness and choosing a strong material. These two factors are the foundation of sag-proof shelf design.

If you cut the length of the shelf in half, it can carry twice as much weight. But now you need twice as many shelves.

If you double the width of a shelf, the shelf can carry twice as much uniformly distributed weight. Of course, if it's twice as wide you might be tempted to put on twice as much stuff, so you haven't gained anything!

If you pick a material that is twice as rigid, the shelf will hold twice as much weight. The rigidity of wood varies a great deal from species to species.

If you double the thickness of a shelf it will be able to carry four times as much weight. A shelf's strength increases by the square of its additional thickness. Making a shelf thicker has a big impact on strength.

Arm yourself for the fight against creep with common sense engineering knowledge about how each dimension of a shelf affects its strength, or rigidity (Fig. A).

The most important dimensional factor is a shelf's thickness. The effect of the other two dimensions, width and length, is straightforward; add 10 percent to the width of a shelf, and it's 10-percent more rigid; add 10 percent to the length, and it's 10-percent less rigid. However, add 10 percent to the thickness of a shelf and it's 21-percent stronger! Strength increases at an exponential rate as you add thickness. That's why wooden joists and steel beams stand on edge. A shelf that's ⅞-in. thick is about 36-percent stronger than a ¾-in. thick shelf. If you're careful, you should be able to get ⅞-in. thick boards from 4/4 lumber. With such a substantial increase in rigidity, it's definitely worth the effort.

Shelving Standards

Let's put our common sense engineering to the test. How wide or long does a cherry shelf have to be to hold up, say, a set of encyclopedias? We can use standard dimensions that have proven themselves reliable over the years to answer this question (Fig. B).

Encyclopedias are large books, so we need a shelf that's at least 12-in. deep. (Books look best when they sit 1-in. or so back from the front edge of a shelf.) How heavy are they? It wouldn't be a bad idea to place them on

Figure B: Standard Shelving Dimensions

Here are some guidelines for sizing shelves that are supported at the ends by brackets. The maximum length of a shelf increases when you use thicker stock and stronger material.

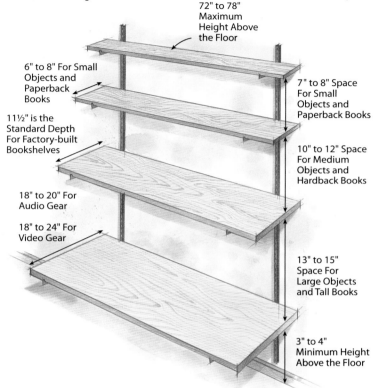

72" to 78" Maximum Height Above the Floor

6" to 8" For Small Objects and Paperback Books

11½" is the Standard Depth For Factory-built Bookshelves

18" to 20" For Audio Gear

18" to 24" For Video Gear

7" to 8" Space For Small Objects and Paperback Books

10" to 12" Space For Medium Objects and Hardback Books

13" to 15" Space For Large Objects and Tall Books

3" to 4" Minimum Height Above the Floor

Maximum length between supports for a moderate load (25 lbs. per running foot) on a narrow shelf (for paperback books and small objects):			Maximum length between supports for a heavy load of 40 to 50 lbs. per running foot on a wider shelf (for large objects, hardback books, and magazines):		
¾"	particleboard	24"	¾"	particleboard	20"
¾"	mdf	28"	¾"	mdf	22"
¾"	plywood	32"	¾"	plywood	30"
¾"	softwood	36"	¾"	softwood	28"
1"	softwood	48"	1"	softwood	36"
¾"	hardwood	48"	¾"	hardwood	36"
1"	hardwood	54"	1"	hardwood	40"
1½"	softwood	66"	1½"	softwood	50"
1½"	hardwood	78"	1½"	hardwood	55"

a bathroom scale and find out. Books and magazines can be surprisingly heavy. These standards suggest they'll weigh up to 50 lbs. per running foot.

How long should a ¾-in. cherry shelf be to hold up these books? The standards tell us that a wide hardwood shelf that carries a heavy load should be no more than 36-in. long. But this doesn't tell us the whole story, and that's why we have to look at one more variable before we can build this shelf with confidence.

How Strong is the Wood?

Some species of wood are much more rigid than others. In terms of deflection under a load, hickory is about twice as strong as butternut. If we make similar shelves out of hickory and butternut, and apply the same load, the butternut shelf will sag twice as much. If we cut the butternut shelf in half, it will sag the same amount as the hickory shelf.

The shelving standards are based on averages. Is our cherry encyclopedia shelf average? No, cherry is more than 10 percent weaker than an average wood like walnut or soft maple (Fig. C). Thus, the shelf has to be shorter or thicker.

Plywood and Composite Woods

Manufactured wood products are not as strong as solid wood. Plywood is only about half as rigid as the average hardwood because it's made of alternating layers of thick veneer. Wood is not as rigid across the grain as along the grain. In a shelf, the

Figure C: Rigidity of Common Wood Species

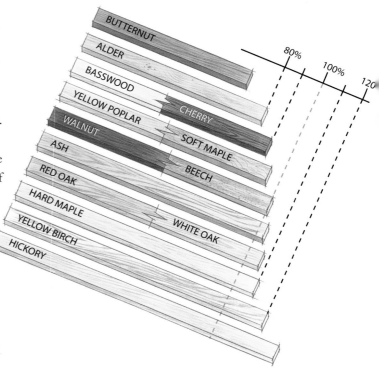

Wood species vary dramatically in rigidity. Standard shelving dimensions are based on using a wood of average strength, such as walnut. To find out how much shorter or longer a shelf of another wood should be, multiply the suggested length by the percentages above.

grain of some of the veneer layers runs the long way, but almost half runs the short way.

Particleboard and MDF (medium density fiberboard), collectively called composite woods, do not have the grain structure of solid wood or of plywood veneers. These products have a hard time holding up their own weight. They have about one-quarter of the strength of an average wood. Nevertheless, composite wood is widely used for shelving. Comprehensive

Figure D: Strengthening Plywood and Composite Shelves

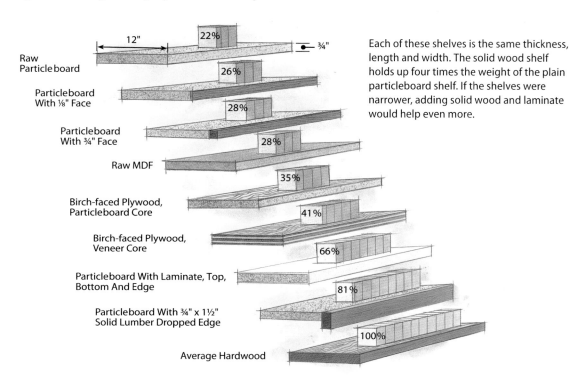

12"   22%   ¾"
Raw Particleboard

26%
Particleboard With ⅛" Face

28%
Particleboard With ¾" Face

28%
Raw MDF

35%
Birch-faced Plywood, Particleboard Core

41%
Birch-faced Plywood, Veneer Core

66%
Particleboard With Laminate, Top, Bottom And Edge

81%
Particleboard With ¾" x 1½" Solid Lumber Dropped Edge

100%
Average Hardwood

Each of these shelves is the same thickness, length and width. The solid wood shelf holds up four times the weight of the plain particleboard shelf. If the shelves were narrower, adding solid wood and laminate would help even more.

information on sizing composite wood shelves is available from an industry trade association.

The rigidity of plywood and composite wood can be improved by gluing on solid wood edges or plastic laminate faces (Fig. D.)

How to Strengthen a Shelf

After weighing the encyclopedias, you may find that they exceed the limits of the standards. In that case, we need to make a more rigid shelf. We could widen the shelf from 12-in. to 16-in., an increase of 25 percent. That would make the shelf 25-percent stronger. It's an option, but for the sake of argument let's say that a 16-in. shelf is too deep for our design. What else could we do?

We could shorten the shelf. Like width, it's a straight percentage reduction. A shelf that is 25 percent shorter will also hold up 25 percent more weight.

A shorter shelf for our encyclopedias isn't going to work, however. With all the supplements added to it, there's more than three feet of books! How about making the shelf thicker? If we've already purchased ¾-in. stock, this option is out.

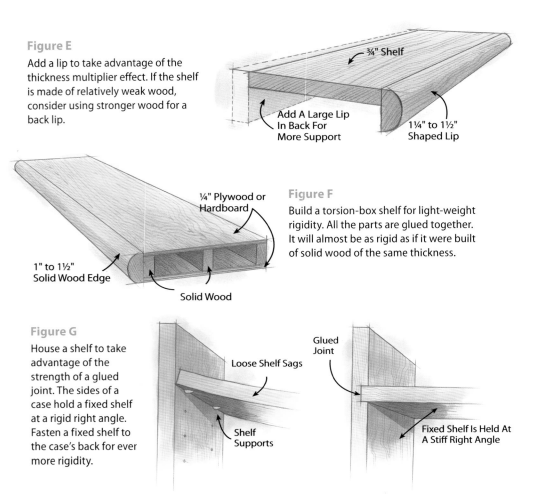

Figure E

Add a lip to take advantage of the thickness multiplier effect. If the shelf is made of relatively weak wood, consider using stronger wood for a back lip.

¾" Shelf

Add A Large Lip In Back For More Support

1¼" to 1½" Shaped Lip

¼" Plywood or Hardboard

1" to 1½" Solid Wood Edge

Solid Wood

Figure F

Build a torsion-box shelf for light-weight rigidity. All the parts are glued together. It will almost be as rigid as if it were built of solid wood of the same thickness.

Figure G

House a shelf to take advantage of the strength of a glued joint. The sides of a case hold a fixed shelf at a rigid right angle. Fasten a fixed shelf to the case's back for ever more rigidity.

Loose Shelf Sags

Shelf Supports

Glued Joint

Fixed Shelf Is Held At A Stiff Right Angle

It's time to be creative about building a shelf that will be stronger than just one solid board. The simplest solution is to add a lip or two to the shelf. Rip some of the ¾-in. stock into 1½-in. wide strips, turn them on edge, and glue them onto the front and back edges of the shelf (Fig. E). If you need considerably more strength, make the rear strip several inches deep.

Another way to add thickness to a shelf without using expensive thick lumber is to make a hollow shelf 1- to 1½-in. thick from thin plywood and strips of solid wood (Fig. F). This type of shelf is based on the engineering principles of a torsion box. It's light in weight but very strong. Use it to carry very heavy loads.

Housing a shelf into the sides of a case will enable the shelf to carry more weight. A fixed shelf is more rigid than a loose shelf because its ends are joined to the sides at a stiff right angle (Fig. G). Some joints are stronger than others, so choosing one kind over another can also effect the strength of a shelf. A plain dado works fine, but a sliding dovetail is stronger because it has more mechanical strength and a larger glue surface area.

Supporting a shelf in the middle strengthens a shelf more than you might think (Fig. H). Weight on one side of a middle support helps hold up weight on the other side, like kids on a see-saw. The net effect is that one long shelf with a center support can hold up more weight than two shorter shelves.

6 Tips for Stronger Shelves

- ■ Widen the shelf.
- ■ Shorten the shelf.
- ■ Use a stronger material.
- ■ Add thickness.
- ■ Add a lip.
- ■ House the shelf ends.

Figure H
Multiply strength by adding a center support. The shelf can then hold up more than twice the weight of two shorter shelves.

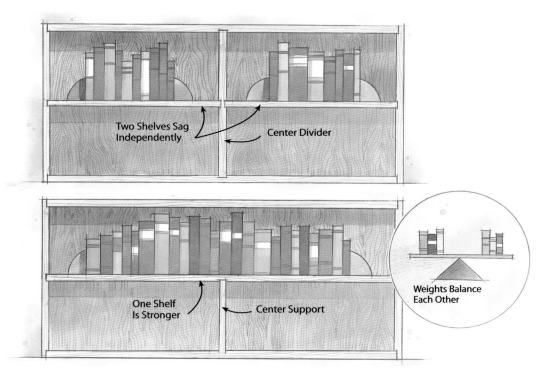

Two Shelves Sag Independently

Center Divider

One Shelf Is Stronger

Center Support

Weights Balance Each Other

by SETH KELLER

Sliding Bookrack

ARTS & CRAFTS DETAILS ADD SOPHISTICATION TO A SIMPLE PROJECT

I 've always admired the work of Greene & Greene, two architects who designed Arts & Crafts homes and furnishings in the early 20th century. Their detailing is exquisite. I love the softened edges, pegged joinery, square motifs and overall lightness of their work. When I needed bookends to hold some special volumes, I turned to these gifted artists for inspiration.

This bookrack works on a very simple principle: friction. The bookends are adjustable, sliding on two rails to hold any set of books. But when you push the ends up to the books, they tilt slightly and bind against the rails. They're locked in place. When you pull a book out, the ends are released and free to slide again.

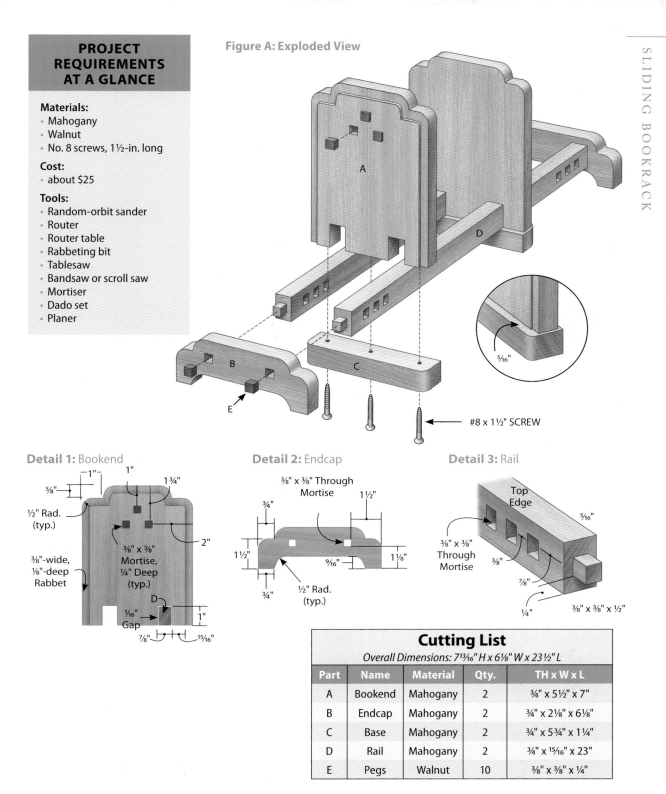

PROJECT REQUIREMENTS AT A GLANCE

Materials:
- Mahogany
- Walnut
- No. 8 screws, 1½-in. long

Cost:
- about $25

Tools:
- Random-orbit sander
- Router
- Router table
- Rabbeting bit
- Tablesaw
- Bandsaw or scroll saw
- Mortiser
- Dado set
- Planer

Figure A: Exploded View

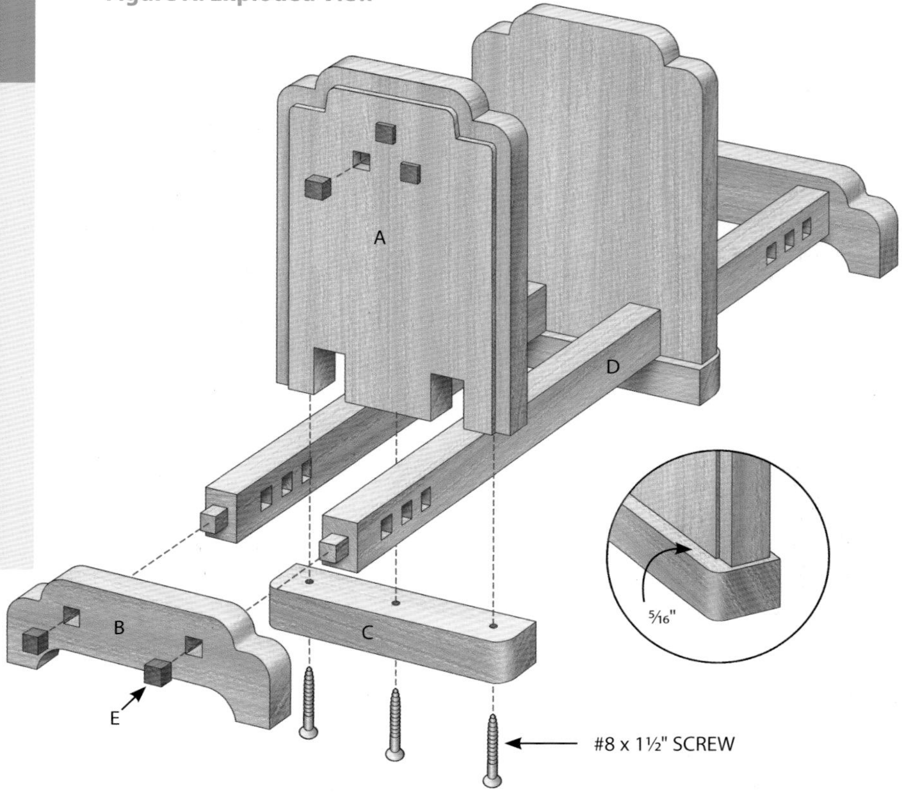
A
B
C
D
E
5/16"
#8 x 1½" SCREW

Detail 1: Bookend

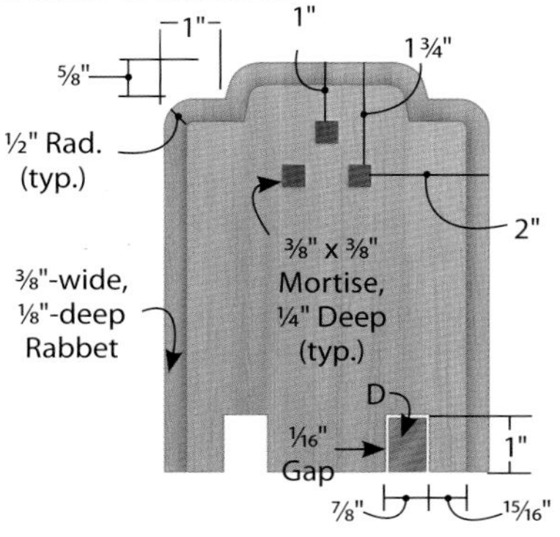
1"
1"
1¾"
⅝"
½" Rad. (typ.)
2"
⅜" x ⅜" Mortise, ¼" Deep (typ.)
⅜"-wide, ⅛"-deep Rabbet
D
1/16" Gap
1"
⅞"
15/16"

Detail 2: Endcap

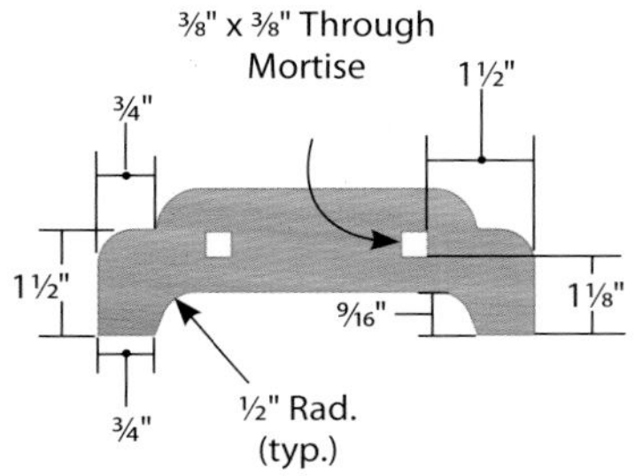
⅜" x ⅜" Through Mortise
1½"
¾"
1½"
1⅛"
9/16"
¾"
½" Rad. (typ.)

Detail 3: Rail

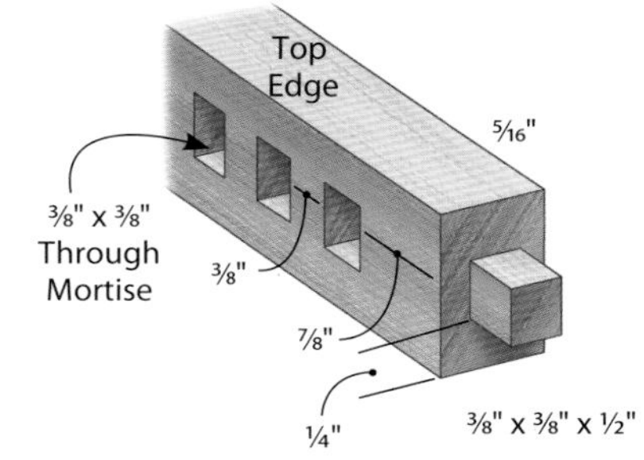
Top Edge
5/16"
⅜" x ⅜" Through Mortise
⅜"
⅞"
¼"
⅜" x ⅜" x ½"

Cutting List

Overall Dimensions: 7 13/16" H x 6⅛" W x 23½" L

Part	Name	Material	Qty.	TH x W x L
A	Bookend	Mahogany	2	¾" x 5½" x 7"
B	Endcap	Mahogany	2	¾" x 2⅛" x 6⅛"
C	Base	Mahogany	2	¾" x 5¾" x 1¼"
D	Rail	Mahogany	2	¾" x 15/16" x 23"
E	Pegs	Walnut	10	⅜" x ⅜" x ¼"

Make the Parts

1. Mill the bookends (A), endcaps (B) and bases (C) to final size. Mill the rails (D) an extra ⅛ in. thick.

2. Cut the bookends, endcaps and bases on the bandsaw (Photo 1; Fig. A). Sand the sawn edges. Use 100-, 120- and 150-grit sandpaper.

3. Rout the bookend profile with a ⅜-in. rabbeting bit (Photo 2; Fig. A, Detail 1). Raise the bit in 1/16-in. increments to avoid tear-out. Use a chisel to square the rabbet's inside corners.

4. Cut shallow mortises into the bookends (Fig. A, Detail 1). Cut through mortises in the endcaps and rails (Photo 3; Fig. A, Details 2 and 3).

5. Plane the rails to final thickness (Photo 4).

6. Cut tenons on the rails using a dado set (Fig. A, Detail 3).

7. Make pegs (E) from ⅜-in.-thick square blank. Cut the pegs to length with a Japanese pull saw, dovetail saw or bandsaw.

Assemble the Bookrack

8. Glue and clamp the rails and endcaps. Work on a flat surface. Check the assembly for wobble before you set it aside to dry.

9. Glue pegs (E) into the bookends and endcaps (Photo 5). Leave the pegs proud by at least 1/16 in. Scrape excess glue from around the pegs before the glue dries.

10. Use 180-grit sandpaper in a random-orbit sander to round the edges of the pegs.

Begin by sawing the sliding bookends and other curved pieces. You can cut two at the same time. Hold the pieces together with double-stick tape.

Rout a stepped profile on the bookends using a rabbeting bit. To safely begin the cut, pivot the workpiece against a starting pin. Once started, you can ride on the bit's bearing.

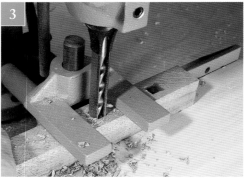

Cut square holes through the rails using a mortising machine. Some tear-out on the back is inevitable, even with a sacrificial board under the rail, but you'll remove it in the next step.

Before Planing

After Planing

Plane the rails to final thickness. Place the torn-out sides facing up. They'll come out perfectly smooth.

Glue walnut pegs into the square holes. The heads of the pegs should be slightly proud of the surface. Round over their sharp corners with sandpaper after the glue is dry.

Cut slots in the bookends. Their spacing is critical for the bookends to slide smoothly on the rails. Assemble the base first; then mark each slot's position directly from the rails.

11. Mark bookend slot positions directly from the rail and endcap assembly. Cut slots with a miter gauge and a tall auxiliary fence (Photo 6).

12. Predrill bases and bookends. Screw parts together on the rail and endcap assembly and test fit. There should be a little play so the bookends slide.

13. Disassemble and sand with 180- and 220-grit sandpaper to gently round all edges, except those on the bottom.

14. Apply the finish. I wiped on two coats of a mixture of cherry and medium-walnut Danish oil.

15. Apply a coat of paste wax over every surface and rub out with #0000 steel wool. This is essential. The wax lubricates the rails, allowing the bookends to slide smoothly.

16. Screw the bases to the bookends. Load the rack with books.

by DAVE MUNKITTRICK

Swedish Wall Shelf

BUILD A CHARMING SHELF IN AN AFTERNOON

It makes a great gift and it's easy to make a bunch all at once. While the design is based on a 19th-century Swedish-American clock shelf, its use today is limited only by your imagination. Kitchen spice shelf, photo display shelf, knickknack shelf—it's great for just about anything, except maybe encyclopedias!

Getting Started

You'll need a scroll saw to cut out the parts for this project. In a pinch a bandsaw could do the job, but you'll have a lot more sanding to do on the edges. Because the parts for this shelf are small enough to fit around knots and defects, you can save some money by ordering a lower grade of wood called #1 or #2 common. We used #1 common butternut for our shelf and paid $1.98 a board foot versus $3.24 for select grade. Plan on three board feet per shelf.

Photocopy the templates in Fig. B, then transfer the pattern to your blanks with a hot iron (Photo 1).

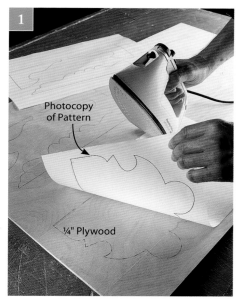

Iron on a photocopy of the patterns using a household iron set on high with no steam. If you're building several shelves, transfer the patterns onto a piece of ¼-in. birch plywood to make reusable templates. Or, for a single shelf, spray some low-tack mounting adhesive on the back of each paper pattern and stick it right onto the wood.

Making The Parts

Lay out the shelf pieces on your wood (Photo 2). If you're thinking of making several shelves at once, stack up to three of your blanks using 1/2-in. square pieces of double-stick tape. Be careful when taking the stacked pieces apart after sawing because the double-stick tape is strong enough to take some wood with it. To avoid any problem, dribble some mineral spirits between the layers to dissolve the adhesive before separating them.

Cut out the shelf parts on a scroll saw (Photo 3). Finish-sand all your pieces before assembly. It's a lot easier to sand flat pieces now rather than trying to get into a bunch of small corners later. Begin with 120-grit paper and work your way up to 320-grit.

Putting It All Together

For maximum strength, the brackets (C in Fig. A) are held onto the wall panel (B in Fig. A) with screws. Nails are used to fasten the shelf (A in Fig. A) to the brackets because their holes are easily filled. Take care when nailing, drilling or driving screws because the shelf parts are thin and delicate. Go slow and use a light touch to prevent splits.

Assembly is an exercise in small-part management. Trying to do without clamps may seem quicker, but you'd have to be built like an octopus to pull it off. The entire assembly can be done with the wall panel lying flat on your bench and using a simple 2x4 as a clamping aid. Here's how:

Trace the outline of your template onto the wood. Take advantage of grain patterns around knots that follow the shape of your piece.

1. Square up the edges of a 2x4 and cut to 7⅝-in., then clamp the brackets to the ends of the 2x4 (Photo 4).

2. Use a tape measure to center the brackets on the back of the wall panel, then mark their location (Photo 4).

3. Turn the wall panel over and center the bracket assembly on the face of the back panel. Place the shelf on your bench so that one bracket overhangs the edge (Photo 5).

4. Drill two 3/32-in. pilot holes and fasten with two #6 x 1-in. screws (Photo 5). To avoid stripping out the holes, drive the screws by hand.

5. Turn the piece around and repeat step 4 for the other bracket.

Figure A: Exploded View

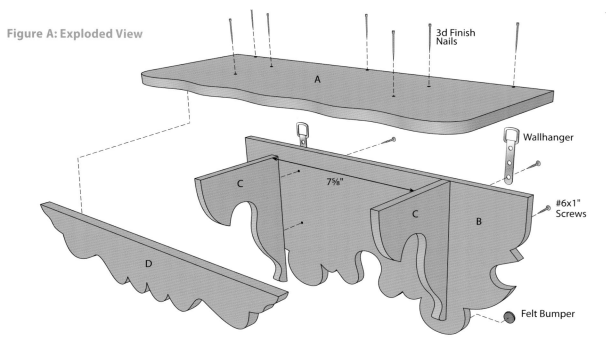

3d Finish Nails

A

Wallhanger

7⅝"

C

#6x1" Screws

C

B

D

Felt Bumper

Cutting List			
Overall dimensions: 7 ⁷⁄₁₆" H x 16" W x 6" D			
Part	Name	Qty.	Dimensions
A	Shelf	1	⁷⁄₁₆" x 6" x 15¾"
B	Wall Panel	1	⁷⁄₁₆" x 7" x 15"
C	Brackets	2	⁷⁄₁₆" x 4¼" x 6¼"
D	Valance	1	⁷⁄₁₆" x 2⅛" x 12¾"

Materials: 3 board feet #1 butternut, approx. $6.

6. Slide the wall panel assembly back onto your bench. Center the shelf, top-side down, on the brackets. Then, trace the bracket's outline onto the shelf.

7. Turn the shelf right-side up and re-center the brackets. Then, use a clamp to secure the shelf to the 2x4 block (Photo 6).

8. Use the bracket outlines as a guide and drill two ¹⁄₁₆-in. pilot holes through the shelf into each bracket. Be sure to place the holes where the brackets are wide enough to

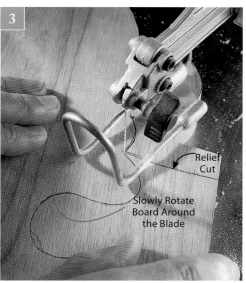

3

Relief Cut

Slowly Rotate Board Around the Blade

Cut out the pieces on the scroll saw. For tight inside corners like this, use what's called a "zero-radius" turn. Here's how to do it: Cut all the way into the corner, then rotate the piece around the blade by letting the teeth slowly nibble away as you complete the turn. If you've never done a zero-radius turn before you can always make relief cuts into the corners to give your blade more room.

accept the screw. Drill three holes along the back edge of the shelf for nailing the top to the wall panel.

9. Run a small bead of glue along the top edge of the back panel and nail the top to the brackets and wall panel (Photo 6).

10. Attach the valance (Photo 7).

Finishing Touches

Use 320-grit sandpaper to do a little touch-up sanding and ease the edges. Now you're ready to finish. We used Watco medium walnut oil for the finish and Behlen Fil-Sticks to fill the nail holes.

Now, attach a couple wall hangers to the back and you're ready to hang your shelf! You just need to find the perfect spot, "...a little to your left...a little lower...try more to the right..."

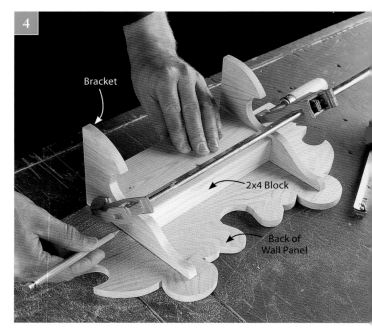

4

Bracket

2x4 Block

Back of Wall Panel

Outline the shelf brackets onto the back of the wall panel. This will show you exactly where to drill the pilot holes for the screws.

Figure B: Templates

Make a photocopy of these templates at 200 percent enlargement (you'll need a copier that handles 11-x-17-in. paper). Then, take the enlargement and cover one of the images with a piece of white paper and photocopy again at 200 percent (400 percent total enlargement). Remove the paper, cover the other image and photocopy. Set the tone scale as dark as it can go without causing gray shadows on the white background. This will ensure a heavy coat of toner for transferring onto your template stock.

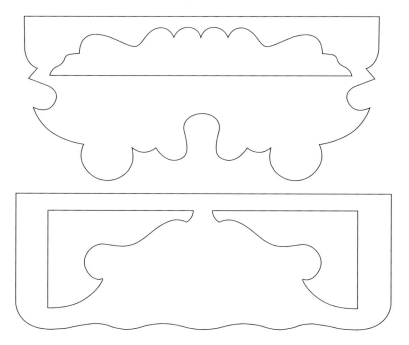

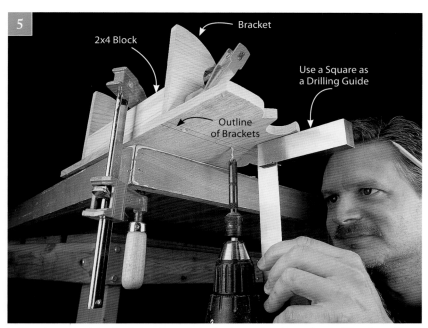

5

2x4 Block

Bracket

Use a Square as a Drilling Guide

Outline of Brackets

Drill and countersink pilot holes through the back panel and into the shelf brackets. Use a second clamp to hold the assembly onto your workbench. Use a square to help guide your drill and place the holes where the brackets are widest (see Fig. A).

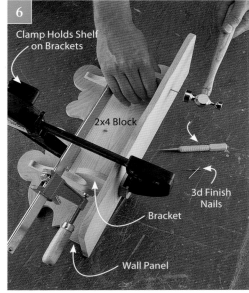

6

Clamp Holds Shelf on Brackets

2x4 Block

3d Finish Nails

Bracket

Wall Panel

Nail the top to the brackets with 3d finish nails. Use a small hammer and tap (don't drive) the nail into the bracket. Use a nail set to countersink the nail heads.

7

Spring Clamps

Oops—Too Much Glue

Valance

Clamp the valance onto the underside of the top with spring clamps. Use a thin bead of glue to minimize squeeze out. A damp cloth can be used to wipe away any excess glue before it sets.

by DAVE MUNKITTRICK

Cantilevered Display Shelves

STRONG, GLUELESS JOINTS SUPPORT THESE ELEGANT, WALL-HUNG UNITS

Whatever you collect—rocks, porcelain, folk art or photos of your Schnauzer—it'll get the attention it deserves when displayed on these shelves. The simple design is wide open at the front and sides so nothing interferes with what's on display. The stepped-back shelves allow ambient light to flood each shelf.

If you're thinking of making some gifts for the holidays, consider these shelves. It's almost as easy to make a dozen as it is to make one. Best of all, these shelves knock down to five easy pieces and six little screws that can be boxed up and shipped to anyone on your list. If you're like me, building these shelves is a lot easier than writing a holiday letter!

All of the curves and tapers make the shelves look tricky to build. But, the joinery is simplified by making all the cuts on square stock before any of the curves and tapers are added. Most of the shaping is done on the bandsaw and tablesaw, followed by a little handwork with a plane or power sander.

The shelves are locked into the supports with bridle joints. The bridle joints consist of dadoes that wrap around three sides of the support. Notches are then cut into the back of each shelf to fit the dadoes (Fig. B). The result is a strong, glueless joint that supports the shelf only at the back.

You'll need a planer, bandsaw, router, drill, belt sander or hand plane and a dado set for your tablesaw. Materials will run anywhere from $25 in pine to $125 in finer hardwoods, such as the figured maple we used here. You'll need about 7 bd. ft. of 4/4 stock for the shelves (this may be the perfect opportunity to use that beautiful board you've been saving for years!) and about 5 bd. ft. of 8/4 stock for the supports.

Keyhole slots are a great way to hang shelves like this on a wall. They're strong, easy to make and the clean lines of the shelves are not disrupted by visible fasteners. Best of all, they don't require buying or fitting any hardware. But, you'll need a specially designed keyhole router bit to cut the slots. Keyhole slots are designed to fit over the head of a screw that's been fastened to the wall. The slot captures the screw head, holding the object securely to the wall.

Start your shelves by cutting your stock according to the Cutting List on page 29. Machine the supports first (Photos 1 through 4) then fit and shape your shelves (Photos 5 through 11). Sand the completed shelves to about 220 grit.

For an easy-to-apply, durable finish we used a wipe-on polyurethane. It goes on like any oil finish but dries fast and hard. For extra protection, apply a coat of paste wax after the oil dries.

These shelves are:
- sturdy
- lightweight
- easily knocked-down for shipping
- fun to make
- easy to mass produce

Make the Supports

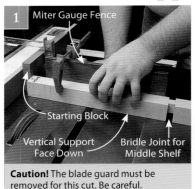

1 Miter Gauge Fence · Starting Block · Vertical Support Face Down · Bridle Joint for Middle Shelf

Caution! The blade guard must be removed for this cut. Be careful.

Cut the deep dado on the front side of the support using a long miter gauge fence and a starting block. This is the first step in creating the bridle joint that locks the shelf onto the supports.

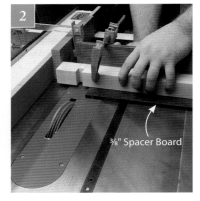

2 ⅜" Spacer Board

Cut the two shallow dadoes on the sides of the supports after slipping a ⅜-in. spacer board under the workpiece. You must cut all the dadoes for each shelf before moving on to the next. That way you keep the same fence and blade setting for each cut, which guarantees perfect alignment of the dadoes on all three sides of the support.

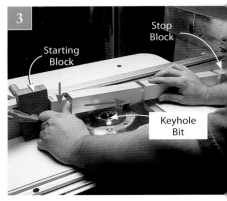

3 Starting Block · Stop Block · Keyhole Bit

Cut a keyhole slot on the back of the supports using your router table and a keyhole bit. Brace the top of the support against a starting block and lower the vertical support onto the keyhole bit until it rests flat on your router table. Slide the support forward against the stop block to finish the cut.

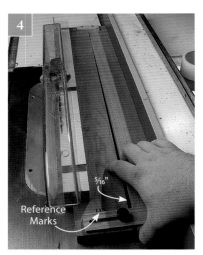

4 Reference Marks · ⁵⁄₁₆"

Cut the tapers on the supports with a shop-made jig (Fig. A), or on a bandsaw. Taper the sides first.
- Set a ⁵⁄₁₆-in. gap between the two halves of the taper jig for the first side cut.
- Set the gap at ⅝ in. for the second side cut.
- Move the fence ¼-in. further away from the blade, set the gap at ¾ in. and cut the front taper.
- Mark each setting on the jig for future reference.

Figure A: Taper Jig

If you plan on making more than one set of shelves, this jig is well worth the little bit of time it takes to construct. Rip a 7-in. x 30-in. piece of ¾-in. MDF into 3-in. and 4-in. pieces. Cut a cradle in the 4-in. piece the same length as the support (24½ in.). This allows you to set the amount of taper by simply measuring the gap between the two halves of the jig. Use ¼-in. plywood to make the hinge and slide. Add a knob and a threaded insert to secure the slide.

Plywood Hinge · 24½" · Knob · Cradle · Threaded Insert

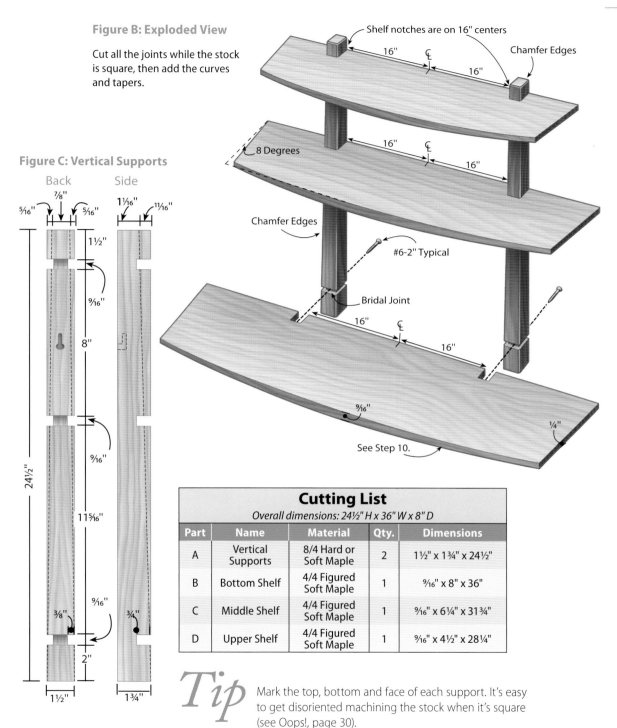

Figure B: Exploded View

Cut all the joints while the stock is square, then add the curves and tapers.

Shelf notches are on 16" centers

16"

℄

16"

Chamfer Edges

8 Degrees

16"

℄

16"

Chamfer Edges

#6-2" Typical

Bridal Joint

16"

℄

16"

⁹⁄₁₆"

See Step 10.

¼"

Figure C: Vertical Supports

Back

Side

⁷⁄₈"

⁵⁄₁₆"   ⁵⁄₁₆"

1¹⁄₁₆"   ¹¹⁄₁₆"

1½"

⁹⁄₁₆"

8"

⁹⁄₁₆"

11⁵⁄₁₆"

24½"

⁹⁄₁₆"

³⁄₈"   ³⁄₄"

2"

1½"   1¾"

Cutting List				
Overall dimensions: 24½" H x 36" W x 8" D				
Part	**Name**	**Material**	**Qty.**	**Dimensions**
A	Vertical Supports	8/4 Hard or Soft Maple	2	1½" x 1¾" x 24½"
B	Bottom Shelf	4/4 Figured Soft Maple	1	⁹⁄₁₆" x 8" x 36"
C	Middle Shelf	4/4 Figured Soft Maple	1	⁹⁄₁₆" x 6¼" x 31¾"
D	Upper Shelf	4/4 Figured Soft Maple	1	⁹⁄₁₆" x 4½" x 28¼"

Tip Mark the top, bottom and face of each support. It's easy to get disoriented machining the stock when it's square (see Oops!, page 30).

Make the Shelves

Plane the shelf stock to fit the dadoes in the supports. Use some scrap to determine the proper planer setting. Try for a slightly tight fit to allow for sanding.

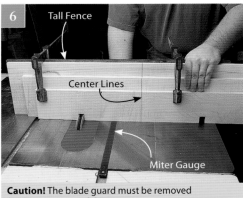

Caution! The blade guard must be removed for this cut. Be careful.

Cut the notches in all the shelves at once. First, make test cuts on scrap to determine the proper width and height settings for the dado blade. Mark the center of each shelf and lay out the notches on the small shelf. Align the shelves in a stack held together with double-faced tape. Clamp the stack to a tall fence fastened to your miter gauge and make your first cut. Reposition the stack, clamp and make the second cut.

Drill and countersink pilot holes for the screws after dry fitting the shelves.

Oops!

Oh man, what a moron! I cut the keyhole slots at the bottom of the supports instead of the top. Now what do I do?

The slots are normally cut when the supports are still square, but now they're tapered. If I cut new slots with the tapered sides I'll end up

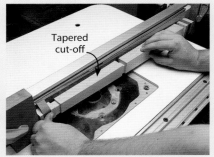

with angled slots. Fortunately, the solution was sitting right in my scrap bin. I fished out a cut-off leftover from tapering the supports and taped it back in place. That gave me the square edge I needed to reference against the fence. Then I cut the slots where they belong, at the top. Maybe I'm not such a moron after all!

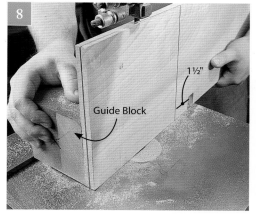

Taper the ends of each shelf on the bandsaw. You want to remove a ¼-in.-thick wedge that ends about 1½ in. from the notch. Use a block of wood as a guide to keep the shelf perpendicular to the table. Stick the block to the shelf with double-faced tape.

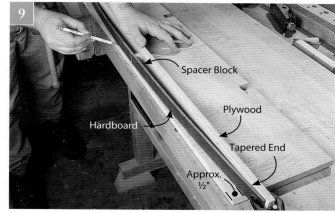

Lay out the curve on the front edge of each shelf. Clamp a ¼-in. hardboard strip on the ends of a 40-in.-long piece of wood or plywood and add a ¾-in. spacer block in the middle. Taper the ends of the plywood to create a fair curve. Cut the curve on the bandsaw.

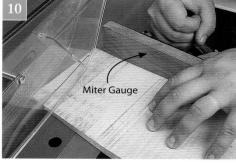

Cut an 8-degree angle on the shelf ends using a miter gauge on the tablesaw.

Installation

Keyhole hangers are about as strong a wall-mounting system as you can get. But getting two screws spaced perfectly on your wall, without leaving multiple puncture wounds, can drive a grown man to tears. After the scars of my first attempt healed (on my ego as well as the wall), I came up with a solution. Take two of those little plastic pushpins for bulletin boards and slide them into the keyholes. Hold them in place with a little tape. Set a small level on the shelf. Position the shelf on the wall, check for level, and push. Voila! The pins mark the exact spot. Hanging the shelves just became a no-brainer.

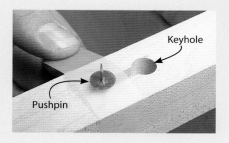

Shape the bottom taper (grid area) with a hand plane or power sander. The object is to create an even ¼-in. thickness across the ends and a sweeping curve on the front of the shelf (Fig. B). Take care not to remove any material around the notch or you'll ruin the fit of the shelf to the support.

by TIM JOHNSON

Floating Shelves

TORSION-BOX CONSTRUCTION CREATES SAG-PROOF SHELVES THAT DEFY GRAVITY

Some time ago, an Ace Hardware ad in *American Woodworker* sparked a surprising number of inquiries from readers. They all wanted to know how to build the cool-looking shelves that appeared in the background. We liked the shelves, too. Their contemporary design and invisible mounting created a dramatic effect.

The secret was torsion-box construction. A torsion box is a simple grid of slender ribs glued between thin plywood skins. It makes these shelves stiff and flat, yet incredibly light. This rigid architecture means torsion-box shelves won't sag or twist, and they can be mounted without any external support.

We've made these shelves easy to build and install by using simple shop-made jigs and dividing the process into four steps. We'll make the torsion boxes, attach the face moldings, then glue the C-shaped units together and, finally, hang them on the wall. To create the wall of shelves shown here, you make four identical C-units and hang every other one upside down.

We wanted our shelves to be a uniform light color, so we chose hard maple instead of birch. The cost is the same, but maple lumber and plywood colors are easier to match. The Multiply brand of underlayment (available at home centers) makes great rib stock, because it's inexpensive, stable and exactly ¼ in. thick. We spent $220 to make our four C-unit shelves.

Build the Torsion Boxes

1. Cut the torsion-box skins (Fig. A, E1, F1 and G1) from ¼-in. maple plywood (see Cutting List, page 40). To get skins for all four C-units from two sheets of plywood, rip each sheet into five 9½-in. x 8-ft. blanks. Cut eight of these blanks into 51-in. and 34-in. skins for the shelves. Cut the eight 18¼-in. skins for the uprights from the remaining two blanks.

2. Cut the sheets of ¼-in. Multiply plywood underlayment into ⅞-in. x 48-in. ribs (A).

3. Plane poplar edging stock to the same ⅞-in. thickness as the ribs' width. Cut the front and end edging pieces (C and D) to width and length.

4. Build the notch-cutting jig (Fig. B).

5. Cut notches in the ribs (Photo 1). Butt the ribs against the indexing piece to cut the first notches. Use these notches to index the ribs so you can cut the next notches, and so on. By using a hold-down, you can cut notches in several ribs at once.

6. Cut some of the long ribs into short ribs that are consistent in length (B, Photo 2).

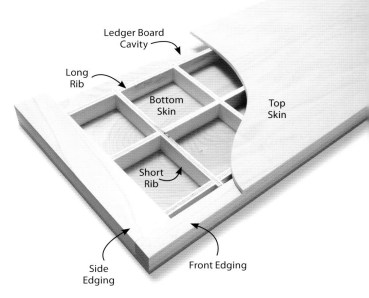

Ledger Board
Cavity
Long Rib
Bottom Skin
Top Skin
Short Rib
Side Edging
Front Edging

PROJECT REQUIREMENTS AT A GLANCE

Materials for four C-units:
- 12 bd. ft. of 6/4 hard maple
- 15 bd. ft. of 5/4 poplar
- Two sheets of ¼-in. x 4-ft. x 8-ft. hard maple plywood
- Two sheets of ¼-in. x 4-ft. x 4-ft. underlayment
- One sheet of ¾-in. x 4-ft. x 8-ft. MDF
- One sheet of ¾-in. x 2-ft. x 4-ft. fir plywood

Cost:
- $220 for four units

Hardware:
- One box No. 9 x 1-in. brass screws
- A handful of No. 6 x 3-in. drywall screws

Tools:
• Tablesaw	• Drill
• ¼-In. Dado set	• Plate jointer
• Chop saw	• Wood glue
• Jointer	• Roller
• Planer	• Clamps
• Router	• Level
• ½-In. Flush-trim bit	• Compass

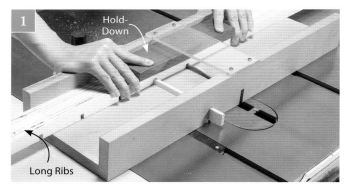

Hold-Down
Long Ribs

Cut notches in the ribs, using a shop-made indexing jig and a ¼-in. dado set. The notches allow you to assemble the ribs into the grid sections that comprise the core of the torsion boxes.

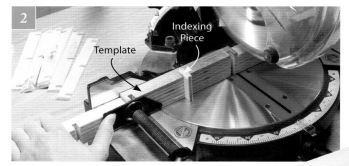

Indexing Piece
Template

Cut short ribs from some of the long ribs. Use a template (Fig. A, Detail 1) and an indexing piece to make sure you cut them consistently.

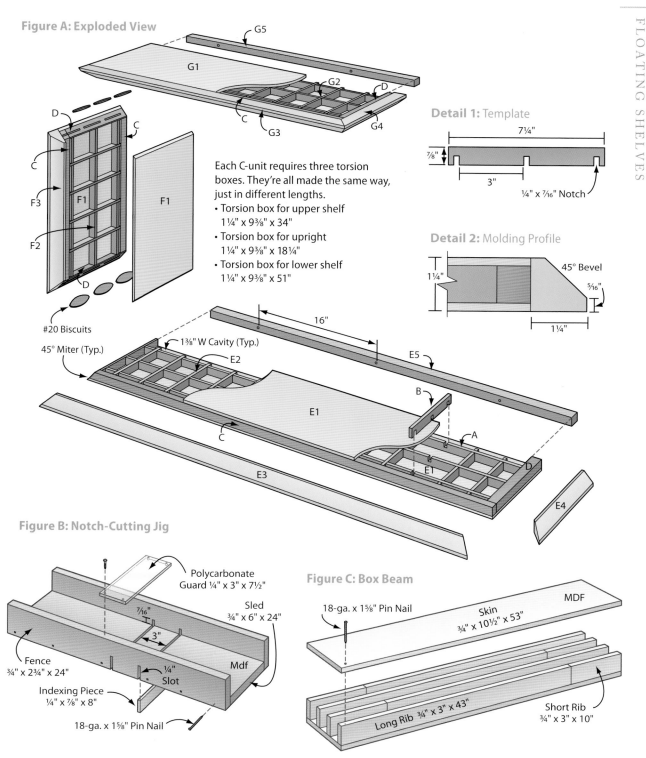

Figure A: Exploded View

G5

G1

G2

D

C

C

G3

G4

D

C

C

F3

F1

F1

F2

D

#20 Biscuits

45° Miter (Typ.)

Each C-unit requires three torsion boxes. They're all made the same way, just in different lengths.
- Torsion box for upper shelf
  1¼" x 9⅜" x 34"
- Torsion box for upright
  1¼" x 9⅜" x 18¼"
- Torsion box for lower shelf
  1¼" x 9⅜" x 51"

Detail 1: Template

7¼"

⅞"

3"

¼" x ⁷⁄₁₆" Notch

Detail 2: Molding Profile

1¼"

45° Bevel

⁵⁄₁₆"

1¼"

1⅜" W Cavity (Typ.)

E2

16"

E5

B

E1

A

C

E1

D

E3

E4

Figure B: Notch-Cutting Jig

Polycarbonate
Guard ¼" x 3" x 7½"

Sled
¾" x 6" x 24"

⁷⁄₁₆"

3"

Fence
¾" x 2¾" x 24"

Mdf

¼"
Slot

Indexing Piece
¼" x ⅞" x 8"

18-ga. x 1⅝" Pin Nail

Figure C: Box Beam

18-ga. x 1⅝" Pin Nail

Skin
¾" x 10½" x 53"

MDF

Long Rib ¾" x 3" x 43"

Short Rib
¾" x 3" x 10"

7. Assemble grid sections (E2, F2 and G2) by fitting the long and short ribs together. These sections don't need to be glued; the half-lap joints hold them together. You'll need two 48-in.-long grid sections for each C-unit. Use one full-length section for the lower shelf. Cut the other into a 31-in.-long section for the upper shelf and a 15¼-in.-long section for the upright.

8. Build a pair of box beams (Fig. C).

9. Glue the torsion boxes, using the box beams (Photo 3). We used Titebond Extend wood glue so we didn't have to rush these complex glue-ups. Lay the edging and grid on the bottom skin and check the fit. The edging should be flush at the front and on the ends. Make sure the grid is snug against the back of the front edging. A 1⅜-in.-wide cavity should extend across the back of the two shelves; the ledger boards (E5 and G5) will occupy this space when the shelves are mounted to the wall. The back of the upright is solid. Roll glue on the edging and grid. It's important to not get any glue in the back cavity. Flip the pieces over, position them and apply glue to the second side. Place the top skin in position. Make sure all the edges are flush.

10. Clamp the torsion boxes between the box beams (Photo 4). Clamp the middle first; then work outward.

11. True up the torsion boxes. After the glue has dried, remove the torsion boxes from the box beams. Joint the front edges, after scraping off any excess glue. Then rip the boxes to the final 9⅜-in. width.

Make the Beveled Molding

12. Mill your 6/4 maple to 1¼-in. x 1⅜-in. molding blanks (E3, F3, G3, E4 and G4).

13. Orient the shelves and uprights for each C-unit and mark the fronts. Mark the open ends of the two shelves, where the end moldings go, too.

14. True the open ends of the two shelves by crosscutting. Remove just enough to leave clean edges. Make sure the cut is square to the front edge.

15. Cut and fit the miter joints on the molding blanks. Then glue them on (Photo 5).

16. Trim the molding edges (Photo 6). It's OK if routing leaves the molding a hair proud. You can sand the surfaces flush later.

17. Rip bevels on the front moldings (Fig. A, Detail 2; Photo 7). To avoid kickback, make sure the blade is tilted away from the fence. Your final pass should leave a $\frac{5}{16}$-in. square shoulder at the top.

18. Crosscut bevels on the end moldings (Photo 8). After your final pass, the square shoulder should match the one on the front.

19. Remove all of the saw marks by sanding the bevels. You'll get the best results if you use a sanding block. A power sander is likely to round over the crisp edges. It's safer to smooth the joints between the moldings and the plywood with a block, too.

Glue the torsion boxes together by sandwiching the edging and the grid section between the plywood skins. This is a complex glue-up, so use glue that won't dry too fast and a roller to spread it quickly and evenly.

Clamp the torsion boxes between box beams. Box beams distribute clamping pressure evenly and guarantee your glued-up shelves will be flat. They're well worth the effort to make.

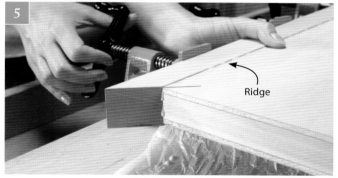

Glue on molding blanks that are slightly thicker than the shelves. Make sure you feel ridges on both sides of the blanks as you tighten each clamp, and again after all the clamps are tight.

Rout the edges flush. Use a second shelf to support the router and a piece of scrap plywood as a spacer.

Bevel the molding. It's difficult to get good results when you cut thick, hard wood at an angle, so make two passes. First, make a slightly oversize rough cut. Adjust the fence and make a second light pass to clean the edge.

Caution! If your shelf and miter gauge are unstable in the starting position because they hang off the front of the saw, use a sled to make this cut.

Bevel the end molding with your miter gauge and a long support fence. Rough-cut the bevel and then make a light final pass.

9

Miter both ends of the upright and the inside ends of the shelves. Unlike the previous beveled cuts, these go all the way to the tip.

10

Cut biscuit slots. Biscuits align and strengthen the miter joints.

11

Clamp the three shelf components together without glue, so you can check the fit of the miter joints. Use plywood braces to support the upper shelf and hold everything square.

Plywood Brace

12

1¾"

Grocery-Bag Paper

Glue temporary clamping blocks at the corners. They'll allow you to clamp the miter joints effectively, without using long, heavy clamps. Pieces of heavy paper glued between the block and the shelf make the blocks removable.

13

Clamp the miter joints to glue the C-unit together. After the glue dries, the clamping blocks knock off easily because of the paper, and the residue cleans off completely with water.

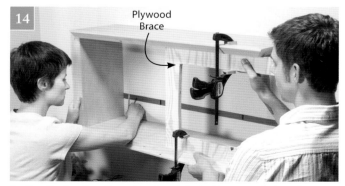

14

Plywood Brace

Position the C-unit on the wall and mark the inside corner. A piece of tape can be used to mark stud locations. Installation is easiest when both ledger boards anchor in two studs.

Argh!

Oops!

My face molding doesn't cover the shelf's plywood edge! The molding was noticeably bowed, and I forgot to check the edges when I was gluing it on. Now I'll have to cut off the molding and start over.

Molding that isn't straight can be a real pain to glue on. The solution is to use a spline. Registering bowed or twisted molding with a spline guarantees it'll glue on perfectly. Cut shallow grooves in both pieces, using your dado set. Be sure to locate the grooves off center, so the spline remains hidden after you cut the bevels.

For both edges of the molding to stand proud, the molding's groove has to be slightly offset from the groove in the shelf. Creating the offset is easy. Make sure the top face of each piece rides against the fence when you cut. First, cut the groove in the molding. Before you cut the groove in the shelf, simply move the fence a bit closer to the blade. If your molding is 1/16-in. thicker than your shelf, a 1/32-in. fence adjustment centers the molding.

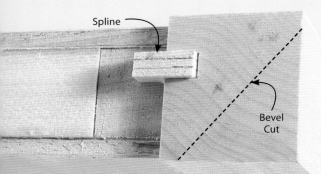

Spline

Bevel
Cut

Build the Mitered C-Unit

20. Miter the corners (Photo 9). These angled cuts won't tax your saw the way the molding did, because the core material isn't as dense. The miters must be dead on, so make test cuts and be sure of three things:

- Your miter gauge slides smoothly, without any side-to-side play.
- Your miter gauge is set at exactly 90 degrees to the blade.
- Your blade is tilted exactly 45 degrees.

21. Check your miter cuts with an accurate square. Cut again if necessary. It doesn't matter whether your shelves end up the same size as the dimensions in the Cutting List. What's important is that the joints fit.

22. Cut slots in the mitered ends for biscuits (Photo 10).

23. Make a pair of fir plywood braces to square and support the C-unit during assembly. The height must match the upright's inside length (between the miters), and the outside corners must be dead-on at 90 degrees.

24. Assemble the C-unit and check the miter joints (Photo 11). Adjustments are easy because the biscuits and braces keep things in place when you loosen the clamps.

25. Glue clamping blocks onto the shelves (Photo 12). Grocery-bag paper and triangular offcuts from beveling the molding are perfect. Be sure to glue both sides of the paper. Don't use clamps; just rub the blocks back and forth on the surface until they stick. Wait at least 15 minutes before using them.

26. Disassemble the C-unit and apply glue to the miter joints. Reassemble the unit and clamp the corners, using the temporary blocks (Photo 13). Be fussy when you fit the joints.

27. Remove the clamping blocks by tapping the end grain with a hammer. The papered joints will break, leaving half the paper on the block and half on the shelf. (You can also split a papered joint with a chisel.) Moisten the paper residue on the shelves to soften the glue. After a few minutes, the paper will rub off and the glue will turn white, so it'll be easy to see. Gently scrub off the glue using a paper towel or a fine nylon abrasive pad. Don't use steel wool; it'll discolor the wood. Remove excess glue from the mitered joints the same way.

Mount the C-Unit on the Wall

28. Mill ledger boards for both shelves. They should fit the cavities firmly, but without binding.

29. Locate the C-unit on the wall after marking the stud locations (Photo 14).

30. Fasten the lower ledger board to the wall (Photo 15). It's shorter than the cavity, for side-to-side adjustment. If you need to be fussy about height, install the ledger a bit below the line, to allow for the shelf's plywood skin.

31. Locate and install the upper ledger board by using the C-unit. It's much easier than measuring on the wall (Photos 16 and 17). It helps to sand this ledger down a bit,

Cutting List for one C-unit
Overall dimensions: 10⅝" x 18" x 52"

Part	Name	Material	Qty.	Dimensions
A	Long rib	Underlayment	6	¼" x ⅞" x 48"
B	Short rib	Underlayment	28	¼" x ⅞" x 7¼"
C	Front edging	Poplar	4	⅞" x ¾" x cut to length
D	End edging	Poplar	6	⅞" x 1½" x 8¾"
E	Lower shelf			1¼" x 10⅝" x 52"[1]
E1	Lower shelf skin	Maple plywood	2	3/16"[2] x 9½" x 51"
E2	Lower shelf grid	Parts A and B	1	⅞" x 7¼" x 48"
E3	Lower shelf front molding	Hard maple	1	1¼" x 1⅜" x 53"[1, 4]
E4	Lower shelf end molding	Hard maple	1	1¼" x 1⅜" x 11½"[1, 4]
E5	Lower shelf ledger board	Poplar	1	⅞" x 1¼" x 47"
F	Upright			1¼" x 10⅝" x 18"[3]
F1	Upright skin	Maple plywood	2	3/16"[2] x 9½" x 18¼"
F2	Upright grid	Parts A and B	1	⅞" x 7¼" x 15¼"
F3	Upright molding	Hard maple	1	1¼" x 1⅜" x 18¼"
G	Upper shelf			1¼" x 10⅝" x 35"[1]
G1	Upper shelf skin	Maple plywood	2	3/16"[2] x 9½" x 34"
G2	Upper shelf grid	Parts A and B	1	⅞" x 7¼" x 31"
G3	Upper shelf molding	Hard maple	1	1¼" x 1⅜" x 36"[1, 4]
G4	Upper shelf end molding	Hard maple	1	1¼" x 1⅜" x 11½"[1, 4]
G5	Upper shelf ledger board	Poplar	1	⅞" x 1¼" x 30"

[1] one end mitered
[2] actual thickness of ¼" plywood
[3] both ends mitered
[4] cut to length after mitering

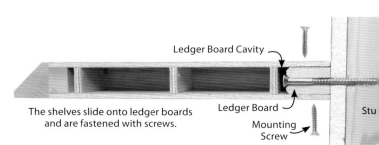

Ledger Board Cavity

Ledger Board

Mounting Screw

Stu

The shelves slide onto ledger boards and are fastened with screws.

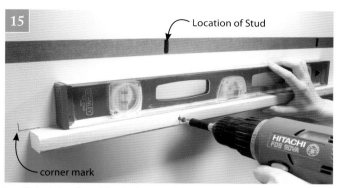

Install the ledger board for the bottom shelf, using a level and your corner mark for reference.

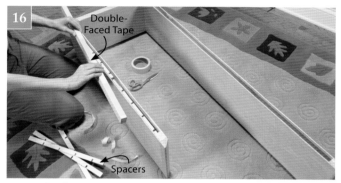

For a perfect fit, use the C-unit to locate the upper ledger board. Attach double-faced tape to the ledger and slide the ledger into its cavity, using spacers so it protrudes. Install the C-unit on the lower ledger and press the upper shelf against the wall.

so it slides easily in and out of the cavity. Use a brace to support the C-unit and keep the shelves parallel during this process. If the upper ledger bridges only one stud, use a toggle bolt for the second anchor.

32. Install the C-unit to determine whether it needs to be scribed (Photo 18).

33. With the C-unit firmly pressed against the wall, drill pilot holes for the mounting screws. Keep the countersink shallow—the plywood skins are thin and you just want the screws to install flush. Fasten the C-unit to the wall (Photo 19). If you're installing multiple C-units, mount each unit separately to drill the pilot holes. Then go back and install them, using a stubby screwdriver to drive the screws where the shelves overlap.

The upper ledger board remains when you remove the C-unit, thanks to the double-faced tape. Anchor this ledger to the studs.

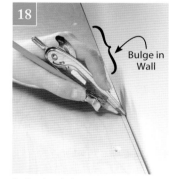

Scribe the shelves to remove gaps. First, transfer the wall's uneven shape with a compass. Remove the shelf and sand the back edges to the lines. It'll be easy because you're sanding ¼-in. plywood skins. Reinstall the shelves. Voilà! No gaps!

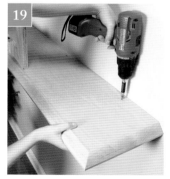

Fasten the shelves to the ledger boards with screws. This is strong enough for most applications and it makes the shelves removable. For maximum strength (to hold your anvil collection, for example) glue and screw the shelves to the ledger boards.

by JON STUMBRAS

Walnut Wall Shelves

VERSATILE GO-ANYWHERE SHELVES TO HOLD ANYTHING YOU WANT

Never enough shelf space where you want it? This little shelf is a great way to add extra storage in just about any room.

It's compact—only 22¾-in. wide by 31¼-in. tall by 9¼-in. deep. Yet it's tall enough to accommodate three shelves of paperbacks. Hang it in your bedroom, bathroom or kitchen. This cabinet gives any room a touch of comfortable elegance.

Details Made Easy

We've packed a ton of great details into this cabinet, and some great techniques into this story. We'll show you how to cut cove molding on your tablesaw and how a special beading bit makes quick work of the shiplapped back. Your router and router table can handle all of the other moldings.

All of the parts for this cabinet are made from ¾-in.-thick lumber, which keeps the materials list simple. An intermediate-level woodworker can plan on two or three weekends to complete this cabinet. And when you're done, a hidden cleat easily and invisibly secures the case to the wall.

Small Changes Make a Big Difference

In a small case, changing dimensions by even a fraction can make a world of difference in the final appearance. The top of this case is ¹¹⁄₁₆-in. thick and overhangs the side by ¼-in. more at the sides than the front. The bottom is ⁹⁄₁₆-in. thick, the shelves are ⅝-in. thick and the face frames are ½-in. thick. These carefully chosen dimensions give this cabinet a comfortable and balanced look.

Traditional Design, Modern Tools

You'll need a surface planer, jointer, router, router table, tablesaw, dado blade and biscuit joiner for the construction. To make the moldings, seven router bits are needed: three round-over bits, a beading bit, a chamfer bit, an ogee bit and a rabbeting bit. You may have several of these already, but if you buy all the bits new, the cost will be approximately $170. We used 25 bd. ft. of ¼ rough walnut for our cabinet at a cost of $125.

Plane your parts to final thickness after you've rough cut them to width and length. It doesn't take long because there are only about two dozen parts.

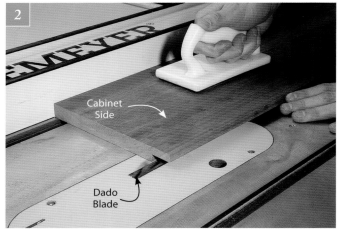

Cut rabbets along the inside edge of the cabinet sides with a dado blade. The cabinet back fits into this rabbet.

Build the Cabinet in Stages

1. Begin by selecting the wood for each part (the sides require the widest boards). Straight-grained wood looks best for face frames. Match the face-frame stiles to the case sides and they'll look like one piece when assembled.

2. Cut all the parts to rough size by adding ½ in. to the final length and width (see Cutting List, page 51) and plane the parts to their final thickness (Photo 1).

3. Next, rabbet the case sides (C1) with a dado blade in your tablesaw (Photo 2). Two passes are needed to make the 1-in.-wide by ⅜-in.-deep dado on the back inside edge of each side.

4. Now cut the case sides, the top and the bottom (C2) to final width and length.

5. Drill the shelf-pin holes next (Photo 3) using a drilling template (Fig. A) and a 5mm self-centering drill bit. It's a lot easier to do this now because there's not a lot of room inside the finished cabinet.

6. You can now join the top and bottom to the case sides. Two #20-size biscuits will fit neatly in the panels (Fig. B). Glue up the case, carefully checking the diagonal measurements to guarantee squareness. Note that the case bottom is set ½-in. up from the bottom ends of the case sides (Fig. B). This way the case bottom and the bottom face-frame rail will be flush on the inside of the cabinet.

7. Make the face frame next. It's difficult to cut accurate biscuit joints in ½-in.-thick material (see Oops!, page 46), so we built a simple clamping jig with toggle clamps for better results (Photo 4). This jig makes it easy to cut the partial biscuit joint (Detail 1) for the bottom face-frame rail (F3), which is only 1¼-in. wide. To cut the biscuit slots

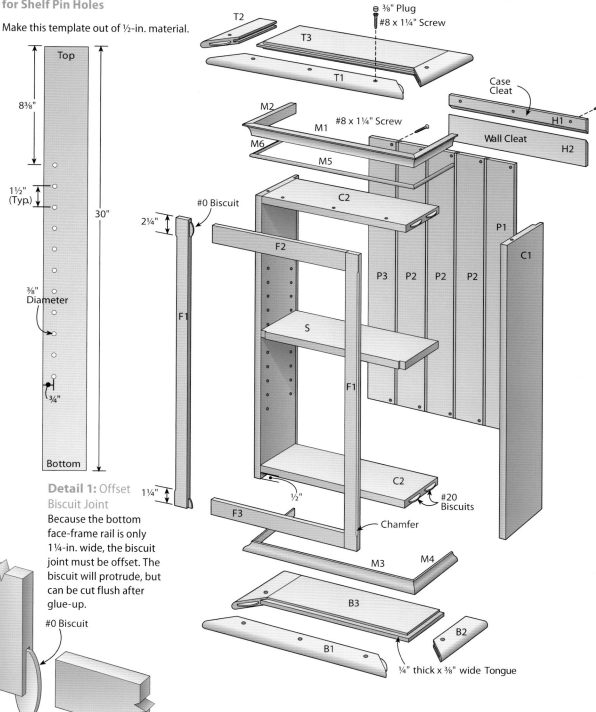

Figure A: Drilling Template for Shelf Pin Holes

Make this template out of ½-in. material.

Top

8⅜"

1½" (Typ.)

30"

⅜" Diameter

¾"

Bottom

Detail 1: Offset Biscuit Joint

Because the bottom face-frame rail is only 1¼-in. wide, the biscuit joint must be offset. The biscuit will protrude, but can be cut flush after glue-up.

#0 Biscuit

Figure B: Exploded View

T2

T3

⅜" Plug
#8 x 1¼" Screw

T1

Case Cleat

H1

M2

M1

#8 x 1¼" Screw

M6

M5

Wall Cleat

H2

C2

P1

2¼"

#0 Biscuit

F2

C1

F1

P3 P2 P2 P2

S

F1

1¼"

½"

F3

C2

#20 Biscuits

Chamfer

M3 M4

B3

B1

B2

¼" thick x ⅜" wide Tongue

in the stiles (F1), modify your first jig, or make a second jig to hold the stiles parallel rather than perpendicular to your biscuit joiner.

Glue up the face frame, making sure it is square. When dry, trim the protruding biscuits at the bottom and glue the face frame to the case (Photo 5). The total width for the face frames is ¹⁄₁₆-in. wider than the overall case dimension. This allows for some wiggle room when gluing the face frame to the case in the event the face frame or case are not perfectly square. The face frame is easily cleaned up with a hand plane, hand scraper, or a flush-trim bit in a router.

8. Next, rout the stopped chamfer along the edge of the face frame (Fig. B).

Oops!

This project taught me how difficult it can be to make biscuit joints in thin wood such as this ½-in.-thick face frame. Thin wood just doesn't provide much bearing surface for the biscuit joiner to rest on. As a result, the biscuit joiner can easily rock or tip, resulting in a poorly aligned joint.

My solution was to build a clamping jig to hold the parts (Photo 4). This also made the process safer and quicker.

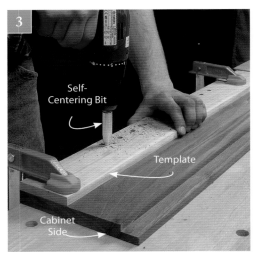

Drill shelf-pin holes before assembling the case, using a template and 5mm self-centering drill bit. The template guarantees evenly spaced holes and the self-centering bit has a built-in stop to keep you from drilling through the side.

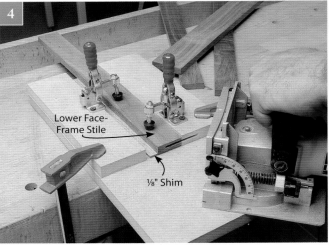

Cut biscuit joints in the face frames. Using this simple jig allows you to safely and quickly cut accurate slots in the thin, narrow parts. The bottom face-frame rail is too narrow to hold a whole biscuit so the slot is offset. The biscuit will protrude but can be trimmed after the gluing and will be hidden by the bullnose cabinet bottom.

Figure C: Bullnose Molding for Decorative Top (parts T1 and T2)

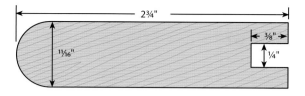

2¾"
11/16"
⅜"
¼"

Figure D: Cove Molding (parts M1 and M2)

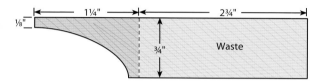

⅛"
1¼"
2¾"
¾"
Waste

Figure E: Bead Molding (parts M5 and M6)

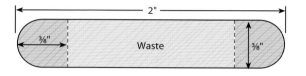

2"
⅜"
⅜"
Waste

Figure F: Ogee Molding (parts M3 and M4)

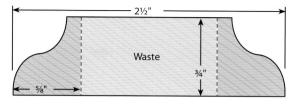

2½"
Waste
¾"
⅝"

Figure G: Bullnose Molding for Decorative Bottom (parts B1 and B2)

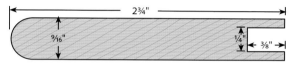

2¾"
9/16"
¼"
⅜"

Figure H: Back Panels (parts P2) Get Routed as Shown Here

Right panel (part P1) has a rabbet and bead on one edge only. Left panel (part P3) has a rabbet on one edge only.

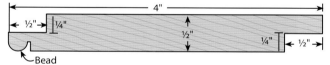

4"
½"
¼"
½"
¼"
½"
Bead

Clamp and glue the face frame to the case. The face frame is 1/16-in. wider than the case to allow some wiggle room during glue up in the event that the case or face frame are a little out of square.

Face Frame

Rout a bullnose profile for the decorative top and bottom moldings with a round-over bit. First rout one side, flip the wood over and rout again. Presto, a bullnose!

Bullnose Molding

Second Pass

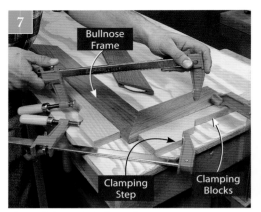

Glue and clamp the bullnose frames one corner at a time. The stepped clamping blocks shown here help pull the miters tight. Make the blocks the same thickness as your parts. First clamp the bullnose frames and clamping blocks to your bench. Then add clamps to the steps on the clamping blocks to pull the joint tight.

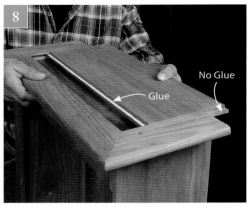

Insert the top panel into the bullnose frame. Glue only the leading edge so the panel can expand and contract with changes in humidity. Wood plugs hide the screws that attach the bullnose frame to the case.

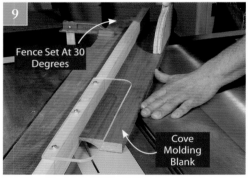

Cut the cove molding with several passes on your tablesaw using an auxiliary fence set at 30 degrees. The auxiliary fence covers half of the blade, producing only the half arc needed for this cove.

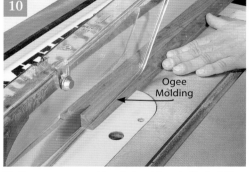

Rip the cove, ogee and beaded moldings to final width on your tablesaw. The cove molding gets ripped once to remove the waste portion while the boards for the ogee and beaded moldings get ripped twice.

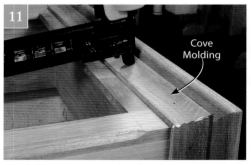

Attach the cove molding with pin nails or small brads. For additional strength, the molding is glued to the case and at the miters.

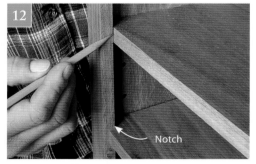

Mark each shelf for a notch before installing the back. Marking right off the cabinet is more accurate than taking a measurement. The notch permits the shelf to slightly overlap the face frame, creating a small, decorative detail.

Add the Decorative Top and Bottom

The top and bottom bullnose moldings (T1, T2, B1 and B2) are made using two round-over router bits (Photo 6). For the top bullnose moldings, use a 5/16-in. round-over bit. For the bottom moldings, use a 1/4-in. round-over bit. The bullnoses will have a slightly flat spot in the center but a little sanding makes them perfect. Cut the 1/4-in. groove (Figs. C and G) in the bullnose parts with a dado blade in your tablesaw. Finally, miter these parts and cut to final length; then biscuit and glue them together (Photo 7). A stepped clamping block is used to clamp this molding together to make a three-sided frame. The frame is then screwed to the case top (Fig. A). The screw heads are hidden with wood plugs.

Next, make the top and bottom panels (T3 and B3) that fit into the grooves of the bullnose trim. To create the 1/4-in.-thick by 3/8-in.-wide tongue on three sides of these parts (Fig. A), use a rabbeting router bit or your dado blade. The panels are 1/16-in. undersized in length to make them easy to slide in. Gluing just the front edge allows the solid-wood panels to move in their frames with seasonal humidity changes (Photo 8).

Make the Moldings

Make the cove molding on your tablesaw. For this cove molding (M1 and M2), set the auxiliary fence at 30 degrees to the blade (Photo 9). A bit of practice is in order here, so start with a scrap 4-in.-wide board for a test run. The wider blank will keep your fingers away from the blade and is less likely to tip toward the blade. Raise the blade in small increments for each cut until you reach the desired depth. When you've mastered a practice piece you're ready for the real thing. After forming the cove, cut the molding to final width (Fig. D). Hand sand or use a curved scraper to remove the saw marks from the inside of the cove.

The ogee molding (M3 and M4) is next. Rout the profile with the ogee bit on both sides of a 2½-in. board (Fig. F), then rip the board on the tablesaw to create two separate moldings (Photo 10). One 25-in.-long board will yield moldings for all three sides.

The bead molding (Fig. E, M5 and M6) is made with two passes of a 3/16-in. round-over bit in your router table. Also, just like the ogee, rout both sides of a wider board for safety and ease of routing.

Using a pneumatic pin nailer makes quick work of applying molding (Photo 11). If you hand nail, it's a good idea to drill small pilot holes to prevent the wood from splitting. These small holes are easily filled and hidden with a little putty or a wax pencil.

Custom Fit the Shelves

Mark the shelf notches directly from the case (Photo 12). The notch should be 3/4-in. long by 1/4-in. wide, but if your face frame was glued slightly to one side, there will be minor differences in the sizes of the notches from one side to the other. Measuring directly from the case gives a custom fit and avoids errors.

Rout the beaded profile for the back. A specialty beading bit makes quick work of this traditional molding. Opposite rabbets on each piece create the overlapping shiplapped joinery for the back panels.

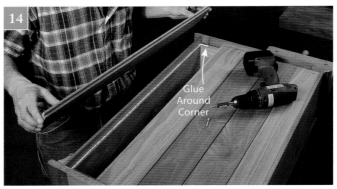

Screw the back panels in place. Gluing the outer two panels along the case sides and 1 in. around the corner adds rigidity to the case. The center three panels, attached with screws, are free to move with seasonal changes in humidity.

Hang the cabinet on the wall using a two-part beveled cleat. One part is screwed to the case and one part is screwed to the wall. Attach the wall cleat to at least one stud and add a couple of wall anchors for extra strength. The cabinet hangs flush against the wall with both cleats hidden from view.

Traditional Shiplapped Back

Rout the beaded shiplapped back panels (Figs. B and H) for your cabinet with a beading bit (Photo 13). Interlocking rabbets allow for expansion and the screws at the top and bottom of each section hold the panels securely in place (Fig. B). Back panels P1 and P3 fit into the rabbets along the case sides. Gluing along the case sides and around the corners provides added strength and stability to the case (Photo 14).

Simple and Classic Finish

To make finishing easier, remove the three center back panels (P2) that are just attached with screws. We sanded our cabinet to 220 grit and applied a walnut stain to even out minor color variations in the walnut. Then we applied a wiping oil finish to give the case a soft glow. An oil finish does not provide much protection against moisture, so if you plan to use your cabinet in the kitchen or bathroom, use a varnish instead.

Hang the Case on the Wall

Attach the case cleat (H1) to the back of the cabinet with screws (Fig. B). Make sure the screws go into the case top (C2). Mount the complementary cleat (H2) to your wall using screws and wall anchors and then hang the case (Photo 15). The beveled cleats interlock and hide neatly within the back side of the case, making them invisible from the outside.

Cutting List

Overall Dimensions: 31¼"H x 22¾"W x 9¼"D

Part	Name	Qty.	Dimensions	Notes
Case				
C1	Sides	2	¾" x 7½" x 30"	
C2	Top & Bottom	2	¾" x 6½" x 18"	
Face Frame				
F1	Stiles	2	½" x 1½" x 30"	
F2	Top rail	1	½" x 2¼" x 16⁹⁄₁₆"	
F3	Bottom rail	1	½" x 1¼" x 16⁹⁄₁₆"	
Top				
T1	Bullnose front	1	¹¹⁄₁₆" x 2¾" x 22¾"	
T2	Bullnose sides	2	¹¹⁄₁₆" x 2¾" x 9¼"	
T3	Panel	1	¹¹⁄₁₆" x 6⅞" x 17¹⁵⁄₁₆"	Include ⅜" wide tongue on three sides
Bottom				
B1	Bullnose front	1	⁹⁄₁₆" x 2¾" x 21½"	
B2	Bullnose sides	2	⁹⁄₁₆" x 2¾" x 9"	
B3	Panel	1	⁹⁄₁₆" x 6⅝" x 16¹¹⁄₁₆"	include ⅜" wide tongue on three sides
Moldings				
Cove Molding				
M1	Front	1	¾" x 1¼" x 21"	
M2	Sides	2	¾" x 1¼" x 8¾"	
Ogee Molding				
M3	Front	1	¾" x ⅝" x 20¾"	
M4	Sides	2	¾" x ⅝" x 8⅝"	
Bead Molding				
M5	Front	1	⅜" x ⅜" x 20¼"	
M6	Sides	2	⅜" x ⅜" x 8⅜"	
Shelves				
S	Shelves	2	⅝" x 6⅝" x 17⅞"	¼"x ¾" notch on each front end
Panel Back				
P1	Right panel	1	½" x 4¼" x 30"	rabbet and bead on one edge only
P2	Center panels	3	½" x 4" x 30"	
P3	Left panel	1	½" x 4¼" x 30"	rabbet on one edge only, no bead
Hanging Cleat				
H1	Case cleat	1	½" x 1½" x 18¾"	45-degree angle on bottom edge
H2	Wall cleat	1	½" x 3" x 18½"	45-degree angle on top edge
Hardware				
Shelf pins		8		5mm shelf pins
Wood screws		23		#8 x 1¼" steel wood screws
Biscuits		12		#20 biscuits
Biscuits		4		#0 biscuits
Wall anchors				appropriate to wall type
Wall screws				appropriate to wall type

by RANDY JOHNSON

Bow-Front Bookcase

SANDWICH CONSTRUCTION AND SIMPLE JOINERY MAKE BUILDING EASY

This bookcase combines straightforward joinery and materials in a design that won't overwhelm your budget or your room. Yet its deep shelves provide plenty of room for oversize books or a place to display your collectibles. The thick, solid look of the center and end panels is achieved with a laminated plywood approach we call sandwich construction. This bookcase is fun to build, so let's get started.

Tools and Materials

You'll need a planer, jointer, tablesaw, bandsaw, belt sander, biscuit joiner, jigsaw, drill and finish sander, plus various hand tools, to complete this project.

We used uniform light birch plywood and select white birch lumber for the main parts of the bookcase. These materials have an overall white/light color. For the top we used flame white birch that has a wonderful figure and grain pattern.

It takes about 2¾ sheets of plywood and 30 bd. ft. of lumber to build this bookcase. The wood costs about $350. If you use natural birch instead, it will cost about half as much to build. Natural birch contains darker heartwood and is what you find on the racks at most home centers.

Start with the Legs

Joint, plane, and cut the legs (A) to final size. Then band-saw and finish-sand the tapered feet (Photo 1). Note that the center legs and the end legs have different sides tapered (Fig. A, Detail 1). The legs are done first because the center sandwiched panel will be made to match the thickness of the legs (Photo 3).

Build the Sandwiched Panels

Saw the plywood parts for the center partition and the end panels (parts B, C and D, and Photo 2). See the Cutting List, page 63, for dimensions and the Plywood Layout (Fig. F) for a recommended cutting plan. Pay attention

Sandwich Construction

Sandwich construction uses readily available thicknesses of plywood to create thicker panels. It also lets you produce a panel with two very good-looking sides because the best side of each piece of plywood faces outward.

There are two basic ways to create a sandwich panel. The first is to simply glue two pieces of plywood back to back. This is the approach we used for the end panels in this bookcase (see photo, below left). This approach works well for cabinet parts that will be fastened to other cabinet parts, such as the ends of this bookcase, which are biscuited and glued to the subtop and the bottom shelf. The reason for fastening these end panels is because the plywood parts that make up the panels are

different thicknesses (¼ in. and ¾ in.), so there is a risk of warping. However, if the sandwiched plywood parts are the same thickness, the chance of warping is greatly reduced. Such panels can even be used where they won't be fastened down, as for cabinet doors or adjustable shelves.

The second way to create a sandwiched panel is to use a center core with a layer of plywood glued to each side (see photo, below right). The center core can be either a lumber frame or another piece of plywood. The lumber-frame approach has the advantage of letting you produce a panel of precise thickness that weighs less than one made with a plywood core. Either core will make a sandwich that is resistant to warping.

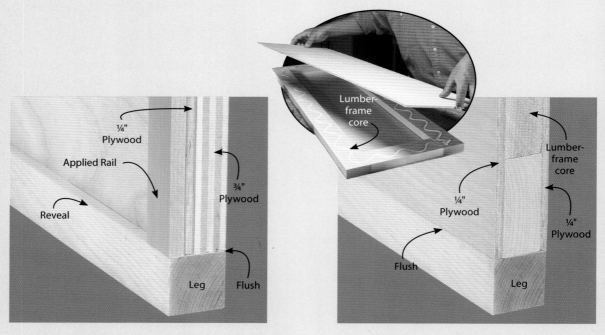

Gluing together a ¾-in. and a ¼-in. piece of plywood creates the end panels for this bookcase. This sandwiched panel is then trimmed to final size, and the legs and applied rails are added. The final result is an end panel that is flush on the inside with a frame-and-panel look on the outside.

Gluing two pieces of ¼-in. plywood over a lumber-frame core creates the center panel for this bookcase. This creates an extra-thick but lightweight panel that is exactly the same thickness as the legs. With a lumber frame on the inside, you can custom-make panels any thickness you want.

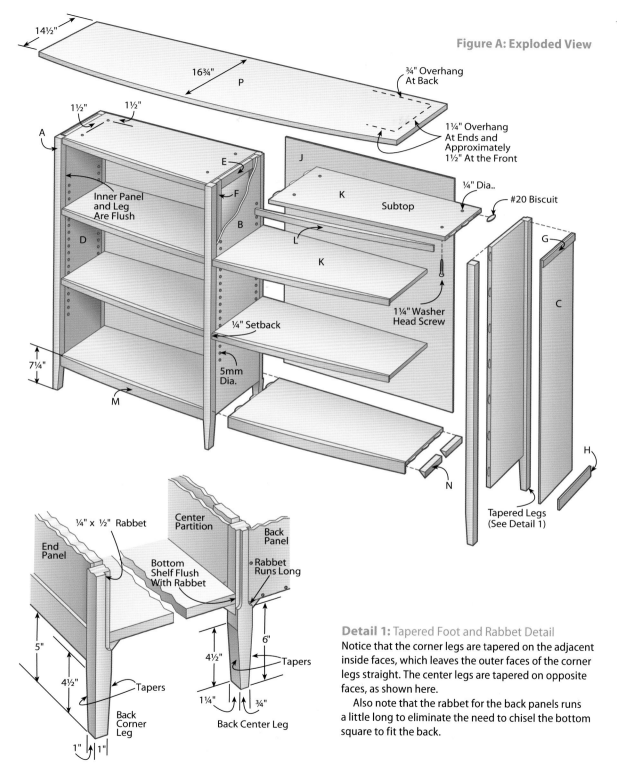

Figure A: Exploded View

14½"

16¾"

P

¾" Overhang At Back

1¼" Overhang At Ends and Approximately 1½" At the Front

1½" 1½"

A

E

J

K

Subtop

¼" Dia..

#20 Biscuit

Inner Panel and Leg Are Flush

F

B

L

K

G

D

C

1¼" Washer Head Screw

¼" Setback

7¼"

5mm Dia.

M

N

H

Tapered Legs (See Detail 1)

¼" x ½" Rabbet

Center Partition

Back Panel

End Panel

Bottom Shelf Flush With Rabbet

Rabbet Runs Long

5"

4½"

Tapers

6"

4½"

Tapers

Back Corner Leg

1" 1"

1¼" ¾"

Back Center Leg

Detail 1: Tapered Foot and Rabbet Detail

Notice that the corner legs are tapered on the adjacent inside faces, which leaves the outer faces of the corner legs straight. The center legs are tapered on opposite faces, as shown here.

Also note that the rabbet for the back panels runs a little long to eliminate the need to chisel the bottom square to fit the back.

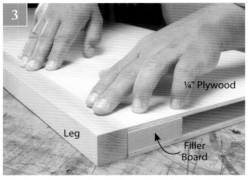

Start by making the legs, because the center sandwiched panel will be made to match them in thickness. After band-sawing the tapered foot at the bottom of the legs, sand the taper smooth.

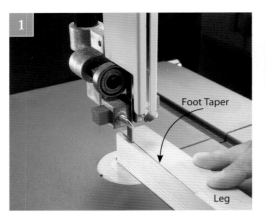

Saw the plywood parts for the sandwiched end and center panels. These parts should be cut oversize at this point. They will be trimmed to final size after they are sandwiched together.

Test the center panel to make sure it is flush on either side of the leg. Adjust the thickness of the filler boards as needed.

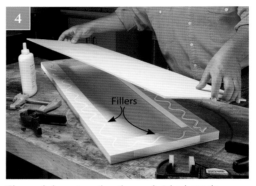

Glue and clamp together the sandwiched panels. The center panel (shown here) uses filler boards. The end panels are just two pieces of plywood sandwiched together.

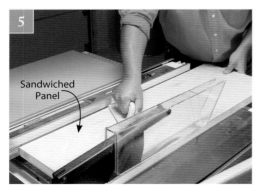

Trim the glued-up sandwiched panels to final width. Cut a little off each edge so both edges are straight and parallel to each other.

Saw the sandwiched panels to final length. This is easy to accomplish with the help of a tablesaw sled. Cut a little off both ends so they are parallel to each other and square to the edges of the panels.

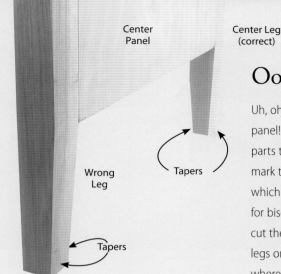

Center Panel

Center Leg (correct)

Wrong Leg

Tapers

Tapers

Oops!

Uh, oh. We glued the wrong leg to the front of the center panel! This is an easy mistake to make when working with parts that look very similar. To avoid this blunder, carefully mark the legs, indicating which ones go on the ends and which ones go in the center. Also, mark which edges get cut for biscuits and glued to the panels, because it's also easy to cut the biscuit slots in the wrong edge of a leg. The center legs on this bookcase have tapers on opposite sides of the leg, whereas the end legs have tapers on the inside surfaces.

to which side of the plywood looks best. You want to pick the best side to face out on the glued-up sandwiched panels.

Next make the fillers (E and F) for the center partition and check that they're the correct thickness (Photo 3). It's tempting to use ¾-in. plywood for these fillers because ¾ plus ¼ plus ¼ equals 1¼, right? Not when it comes to plywood. Plywood is often ¹⁄₃₂ in. or thinner than its specified thickness. This can have a noticeable effect on the final thickness of a sandwiched panel.

Proceed with gluing together the plywood parts that form the sandwiched center and end panels (Photo 4). When the glue is dry, trim the sandwiched panels to final size (Photos 5 and 6).

Add the Legs

Use biscuits and glue to attach the legs to the sandwiched panels (Fig. A, Photos 7 and 8). Pay close attention to the orientation of the tapered foot on the legs when you are cutting the biscuit slots (Fig. A, Detail 1).

It's easy to make a mistake here and cut slots in the wrong face of the legs (see Oops!, above). Also note that the legs are flush with both sides of the center panel but are flush only with the inside of the end panels.

After the legs are attached to the end panels, add the applied top and bottom rails (parts G and H, Fig. A). Complete the three panels by routing the rabbets in the back legs (Photo 9 and Detail 1). The ¼-in. plywood backs (J) will fit into these rabbets once the case is assembled.

Make the Curved Shelves

The curved front shelves and subtops start out as rectangular plywood parts (K) and are tapered on the front edge using a tapering sled (Fig. B) on your tablesaw (Photo 10). To make left and right tapers on the same sled, cut four of these parts best-side up and four best-side down. This gives you three left shelves and three right shelves, all with their best side up, plus a left and right subtop.

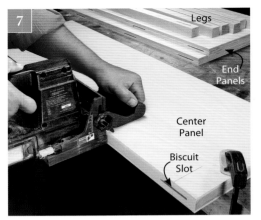

Cut slots for biscuits in the edges of the panels and the corresponding sides of the legs. The biscuits help keep the legs and panels aligned when they are glued together.

Glue and clamp the legs to the panels. The center panel is flush on both sides of the legs but the end panels are flush only to the inside of the legs. It's not necessary to put glue on the biscuits since they are mainly for alignment.

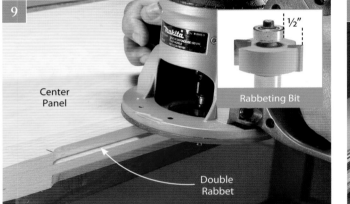

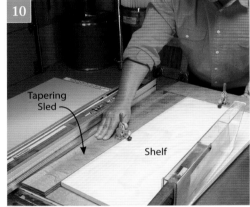

Rout the rabbets in the back of the rear legs. The plywood back fits into this rabbet once the case is assembled. The center leg gets two rabbets and the side legs get only one rabbet.

Taper the front edge on the shelves using a tablesaw tapering sled. This is necessary because the bowed front of the bookcase makes the shelves wider at one end than the other.

Glue the solid-wood edging (L and M) to the tapered edge of the shelves and subtops (Photo 11 and Fig. C). Pay attention that the edging is flush with the good (top) side of the shelves. It doesn't matter which face the edging overhangs on the subtops, just be sure you make one left and one right. Use the curved tracing jig (Fig. D) as a guide to draw the curves on the bottom of the edging of the shelves and

subtop (Photo 12). Band-saw and sand the edging to final shape (Photos 13 and 14).

Assemble the Bookcase in Stages

Start by cutting biscuit slots in the ends of the bottom shelves and subtops, and the joining surfaces of the center and end panels (Fig. A). Make the shelves flush with the rabbet at the back of the legs

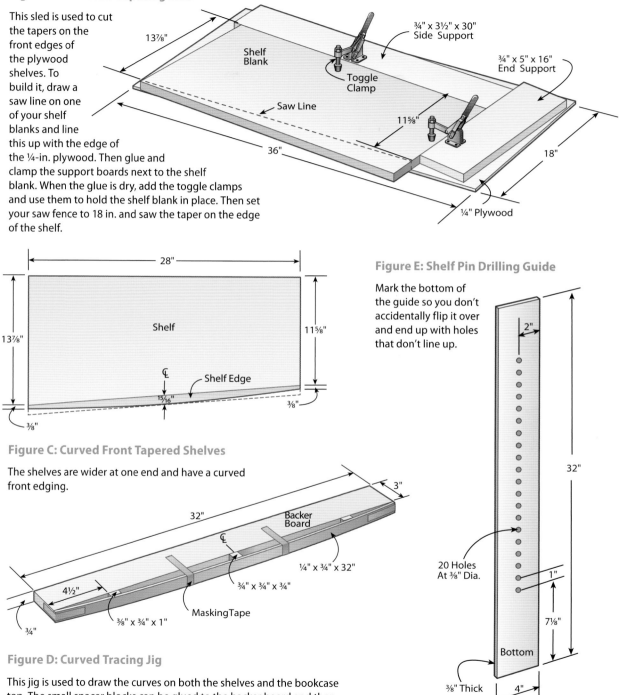

Figure B: Tablesaw Tapering Sled

This sled is used to cut the tapers on the front edges of the plywood shelves. To build it, draw a saw line on one of your shelf blanks and line this up with the edge of the ¼-in. plywood. Then glue and clamp the support boards next to the shelf blank. When the glue is dry, add the toggle clamps and use them to hold the shelf blank in place. Then set your saw fence to 18 in. and saw the taper on the edge of the shelf.

13⅞"

¾" x 3½" x 30"
Side Support

Shelf Blank

Toggle Clamp

¾" x 5" x 16"
End Support

Saw Line

11⅝"

36"

18"

¼" Plywood

28"

Shelf

13⅞"

11⅝"

Ⅎ

Shelf Edge

15⁄16"

⅜"

⅜"

Figure E: Shelf Pin Drilling Guide

Mark the bottom of the guide so you don't accidentally flip it over and end up with holes that don't line up.

2"

32"

20 Holes
At ⅜" Dia.

1"

7⅛"

Bottom

⅜" Thick

4"

Figure C: Curved Front Tapered Shelves

The shelves are wider at one end and have a curved front edging.

3"

32"

Backer Board

Ⅎ

¼" x ¾" x 32"

¾" x ¾" x ¾"

4½"

Masking Tape

⅜" x ¾" x 1"

¾"

Figure D: Curved Tracing Jig

This jig is used to draw the curves on both the shelves and the bookcase top. The small spacer blocks can be glued to the backer board and then the thin wood strip can be held in place with masking tape.

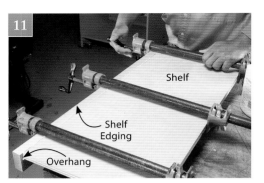

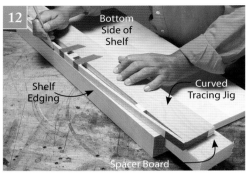

Attach the solid-wood edge to the shelves and subtops. Let the ends of the wood edging run a little long. After the glue is dry, use a handsaw to trim the overhanging ends flush with the ends of the shelves.

Use a tracing jig to draw a curved line on the bottom side of the shelf edging. Drawing it on the bottom side makes band-sawing easier (Photo 13). Use a spacer board to support the tracing jig while drawing.

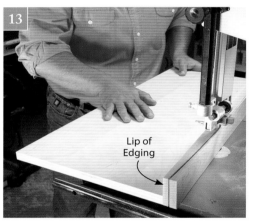

Use a bandsaw to cut the curve into the shelf edging with the lip of the edging pointing up.

Sand the curved edging smooth. Start with a belt sander and finish up with an orbital sander or by hand.

(Detail 1) and set back ¼ in. from the front of the legs (Fig. A).

Gluing and clamping these parts together is a two-stage process (Photos 15 and 16). Practice each stage without glue. Make sure the parts line up correctly. Get a helper to assist with holding the parts. Make sure the case is square before leaving it to dry.

After the glued case is dry, flip it over on its top and add glue blocks (N) to the under side (Photo 17). Glue blocks add strength

to the case. After the glue is dry, turn the cabinet right-side up and drill the shelf-pin holes using a self-centering bit and a shop-made drilling guide (Photo 18 and Fig. E).

Take the four remaining shelves back to the tablesaw and cut ¹⁄₁₆ in. off one end of each shelf. It doesn't matter which end, because you're providing clearance so they're easy to install and remove. A regular tablesaw sled makes this step easy and safe. Add a ¼-in. plywood spacer under the

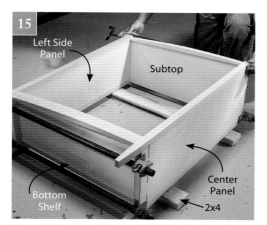

15

Left Side Panel

Subtop

Bottom Shelf

Center Panel

2x4

Glue and clamp together one half of the bookcase first. It's a good idea to test-assemble these parts before you use glue. Propping up the cabinet on a couple of 2x4s makes it easy to check that the parts are correctly aligned on the back edges.

16

Add the second section of the bookcase once the glue in the first section is completely dry. Again, check that everything is square before leaving it to dry.

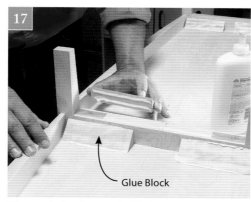

17

Glue Block

Flip over the bookcase and add glue blocks to the bottom. They add an extra measure of rigidity and strength to the legs and case.

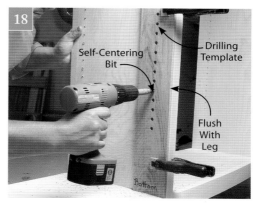

18

Self-Centering Bit

Drilling Template

Flush With Leg

Bottom

Drill 5mm holes for the shelf pins using a self-centering bit and a drilling template. Align the template flush with the front legs and the rabbets at the rear.

bottom of the shelf to accommodate the overhang of the edging and cut the shelves good-side up. This way, any chipping will be on the shelf's under side.

Complete this phase by attaching the plywood back panels (J) (Photo 19).

Make the Solid-Wood Top

After selecting boards for the curved top (P), plane them to thickness and joint the edges square. Use boards long and wide enough to produce a glued-up top about 1 in. oversize in length and width. Cut the top to final size after these boards are glued together.

Cut biscuit slots about every 6 in. along the joining edges. Keep the slots in a few inches from the ends so you don't expose them when trimming the top to final length. Biscuits help keep the boards

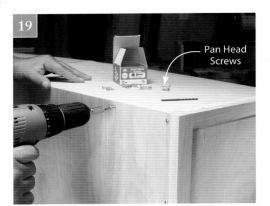

Attach the back with pan head screws. Drilling pilot holes first makes driving the screws a lot easier. The back is now removable, which makes finishing easier later on.

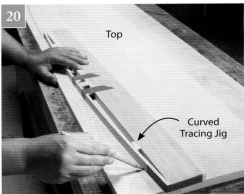

Draw the curve on the top of the bookcase using the same tracing jig you used for the shelves. Draw one side of the curve first and then the other.

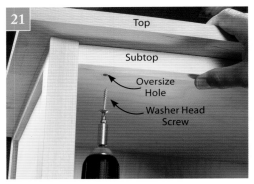

Attach the top using washer head screws. The holes in the subtop are oversize to allow for seasonal movement of the solid-wood top.

Disassemble the bookcase and finish it with your favorite finish. A clear satin vanish looks great on white birch.

aligned, but don't expect flush joints everywhere. You will likely have a few ridges requiring scraping or sanding. Don't worry if the top develops a little twist after gluing. Our top ended up about ½-in. high at one corner but easily pulled flat when we screwed it onto the bookcase.

After you have the boards for the top glued up, cut to final length. Mark the final width at the middle and ends; use the tracing jig to draw the curve (Photo 20).

Cut the curve with a jigsaw and sand it smooth. Attach the top to the subtop with washer head screws (Photo 21).

Finishing

Now that you have the bookcase together, take it apart for finishing (Photo 22). Remove the top, adjustable shelves and backs. This makes finishing easier and reassembly simple, because you know all the parts fit.

Washer head screws are commonly used to attach drawer fronts to drawer boxes, but they also work great for attaching tops to cabinets. The large washer head holds tight without digging into the plywood. Once you've tried them you'll find many uses for them. They're available in 1¼, 1½ and 1¾ in. lengths.

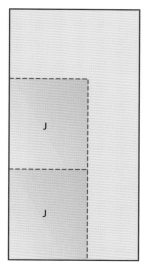

Figure F: Plywood Layout

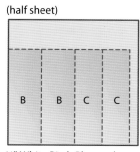

J
J
¼" White Birch Plywood
(half sheet)
B
B
C
C
¼" White Birch Plywood
K K
K K K
K K K
¾" White Birch Plywood
(quarter sheet)
D
D
¾" White Birch Plywood

Cutting List

Overall dimensions: 62¼" W x 42" H x 16¾" D

Part	Name	Material	Qty	Dimensions			Notes
				T	W	L	
A	Legs	6/4 birch	6	1¼"	1¼"	41¼"	
B	Center partition panels	birch plywood	2	¼"	12¼"	36¼"	Add ½" to width and length for rough sawing
C	Outer end panels	birch plywood	2	¼"	10"	36¼"	Add ½" to width and length for rough sawing
D	Inner end panels	birch plywood	2	¾"	10"	36¼"	Add ½" to width and length for rough sawing
E	Short filler boards	birch	2	⅞"	2½"	7¼"	Plane thickness to fit (see Photo 3)
F	Long filler boards	birch	2	⅞"	2½"	36¼"	Plane thickness to fit (see Photo 3)
G	Applied top rails	birch	2	5⁄16"	1"	10"	Plane thickness to be flush with side of legs
H	Applied bottom rails	birch	2	5⁄16"	2¼"	10"	Plane thickness to be flush with side of legs
J	Back panels	birch plywood	2	¼"	29"	34¾"	
K	Tapered shelves and subtops	birch plywood	8	¾"	14"	28"	Finished width is 13⅞" at wide end and 11⅝" at narrow end
L	Edging for shelves and subtop	5/4 birch	6	1"	1"	29"	Rough length, trim to final length after
M	Edging for bottom shelves	5/4 birch	2	1"	2¼"	29"	Glue to shelves and subtops
N	Glue blocks	5/4 birch	8	1"	1"	3½"	
P	Curved top	4/4 flame birch	1	¾"	16¾"	62¼"	Glue up from narrower boards

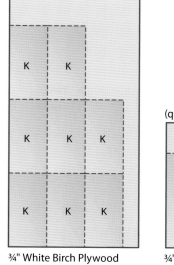

by RANDY JOHNSON

Contemporary Bookcase

FRESH, CLEAN LINES, SIMPLE, STRONG CONSTRUCTION, AND A VERSATILE DESIGN

A strong, simple design with lots of possibilities. This bookcase is extremely strong and sturdy, thanks to double-layered plywood construction and hidden threaded assembly rods. This knockdown, modular design can easily be modified so you can make a bookcase to fit any room in your house.

The credo of many great 20th-century architects was "Form Follows Function." And for this bookcase, it certainly does. The strong shelves are supported in a straightforward fashion by equally strong uprights. No decoration, no superfluous details, not even a back to mar its perfect geometry.

For you, the woodworker, this bookcase has beauty of a different kind. The joinery is amazingly simple: Long threaded rods are concealed inside the pieces and tie the whole bookcase together. There are no angles to cut, no mortises, no traditional joinery of any kind. And finishing is a breeze because all of the parts are finished separately before they're put together. You can buy all of the wood and hardware at a home center for less than $200.

For tools you'll need a tablesaw, dado blade, jigsaw, sliding miter saw, planer, jointer, drill press, hand drill, router and router table. If you don't have a sliding miter saw for the wide crosscuts (Photo 11) use a tablesaw sled instead.

Laminate the Plywood

The backbone of this bookcase is the laminated plywood parts. They make it strong and stiff and give it the look of solid wood. The laminations also provide an easy hiding place for the threaded rods that hold the parts together.

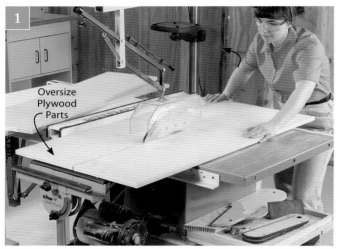

1

Oversize Plywood Parts

Cut all of the plywood parts oversize. Leave the plywood for the vertical partitions (parts L, M and R) as long panels (see Fig. F). The individual vertical partitions are cut to final width and length later. Add ½ in. to the width and length of the shelves (parts A) which are also cut to final size later.

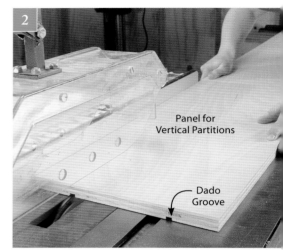

2

Panel for Vertical Partitions

Dado Groove

Make room for the threaded rods that hold the parts together by dadoing grooves into the backside of the vertical partition panels (parts L, M and R). See Fig. B for placement of grooves. When the panels are sandwiched together, the grooves create holes for the threaded rods.

3

2" Long Pegs

Caul

Glue together the panel halves for the vertical partitions (parts L, M and R). We glued up all three pairs at once to help keep them flat. This is a big glue up, so use a slow-drying glue. Use ⁵⁄₁₆-in.-square wood pegs at both ends to keep the panels aligned. The pegs get drilled out later. Use clamping cauls to protect your plywood. If you don't have enough clamps, you can precut your panels in half and glue them up as shorter sections. (Use square alignment pegs in both ends of these shorter panels, too.) This is also the time to glue and clamp the plywood for the shelves (parts A).

Figure A: Exploded View of Bookcase

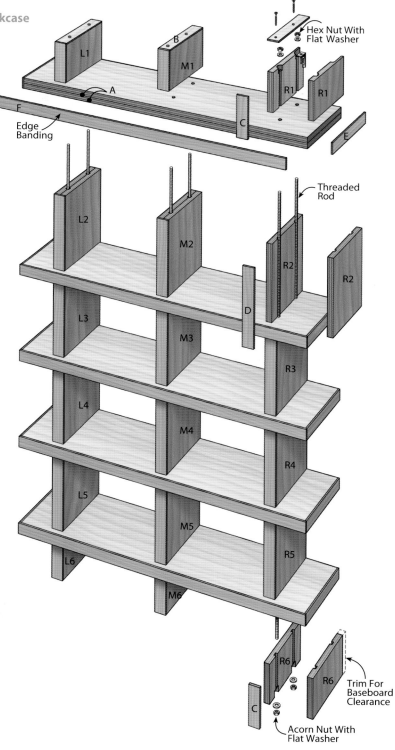

Individual labels on all of the parts make it easy to rematch the wood grain during final assembly.

Hex Nut With Flat Washer

Edge Banding

Threaded Rod

Trim For Baseboard Clearance

Acorn Nut With Flat Washer

Mark and Cut the Parts

Carefully mark and label the individual vertical partition parts. We used a special labeling system that makes it easy to rematch the grain during final assembly.

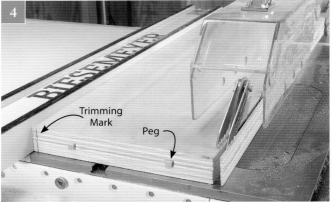

Trimming Mark

Peg

Right Partitions

Left Partitions

Trim the glued-up panels to final width. Measure and cut carefully so the holes are equally spaced from each trimmed edge (Fig. B). Scrape off any glue drips from the plywood edges before cutting to prevent the drips from hanging-up on the saw fence. Also, this is the time to trim the plywood shelves to final width.

Label the individual vertical partitions (parts L, M and R) on the long panels. The markings help you rematch the grain during final assembly. Use the letters L, M and R for left, middle and right and number from the top down. The double lines represent the location of the shelves and will be cut away when the sections are sawn apart.

Figure B: End View of Vertical Partitions

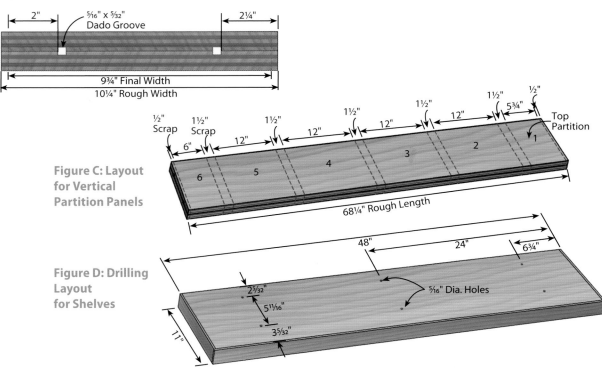

2"

$\frac{5}{16}$" x $\frac{5}{32}$"
Dado Groove

2¼"

9¾" Final Width

10¼" Rough Width

½" Scrap

1½" Scrap

6"

12"

1½"

12"

1½"

12"

1½"

12"

1½"

1½"

5¾"

½"

Top Partition

6

5

4

3

2

1

Figure C: Layout for Vertical Partition Panels

68¼" Rough Length

48"

24"

6¾"

Figure D: Drilling Layout for Shelves

2⁵⁄₃₂"

5¹¹⁄₁₆"

$\frac{5}{16}$" Dia. Holes

3⁵⁄₃₂"

11"

Rough cut the long panels into two parts so they're easier to handle and edge band. Use spacer blocks to provide clearance for your jigsaw blade. Your sliding miter saw would also work for this rough cutting.

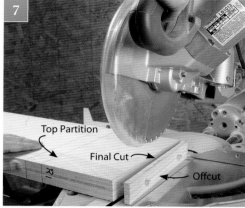

Trim the top end of the vertical partitions to final length (parts L1, M1 and R1). Cut the glued-up shelf panels (parts A) to final length at this time also. A sliding miter saw is a great tool for this job because it's quick and accurate. Prescore the plywood to reduce veneer chipping (see Oops!, below).

Figure E: Cut-Away Detail of Top Partition

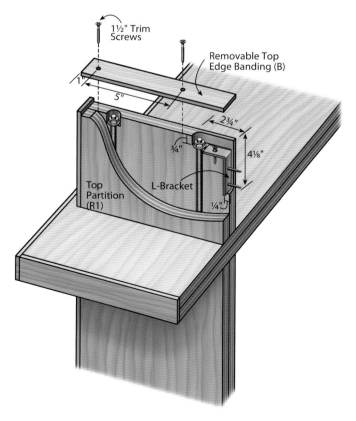

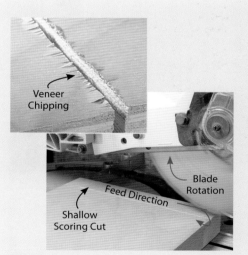

Oops!

Don't let chipped plywood veneer ruin a good day in the shop. Take preemptive action by prescoring the top side of your plywood. Make the scoring cut about ⅛-in. deep on the pull stroke and then, with a return push stroke, complete the crosscut. This reduces or eliminates most veneer chipping.

Edge Band the Plywood

Edge banding covers the edges of plywood and makes the panels look almost like solid-wood planks. Make the ¼-in.-thick edge banding by resawing ¾-in. thick by 1¾-in.-wide lumber in half. Remove the saw marks and reduce the stock to ¼-in. thickness with a planer.

Caul

Edge-Banding Overhang

Cut slots for biscuits in the edges of the panels and the corresponding sides of the legs. The biscuits help keep the legs and panels aligned when they are glued together.

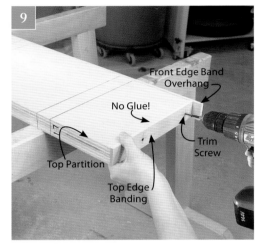

Front Edge Band Overhang

No Glue!

Top Partition

Trim Screw

Top Edge Banding

Glue and clamp the legs to the panels. The center panel is flush on both sides of the legs but the end panels are flush only to the inside of the legs. It's not necessary to put glue on the biscuits since they are mainly for alignment.

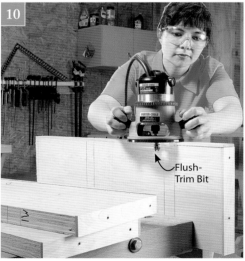

Flush-Trim Bit

Rout the rabbets in the back of the rear legs. The plywood back fits into this rabbet once the case is assembled. The center leg gets two rabbets and the side legs get only one rabbet.

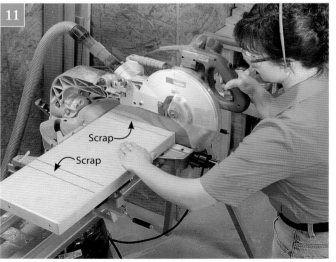

Scrap

Scrap

Crosscut all vertical partitions (parts L, M and R) to final length.

Figure F: Plywood Layout

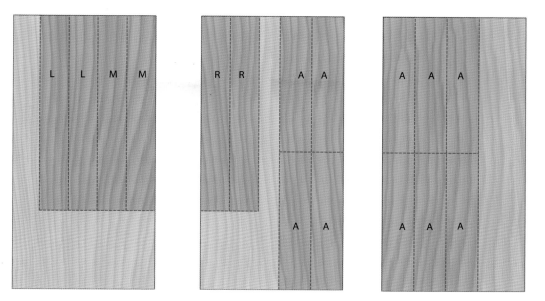

Make It Big
or Make It Small

Want to fill your whole wall (even around a window!) with enough storage for a whole library? You can do that!

The shelves of our bookcase can easily be made longer than 8 ft. by staggering the plywood pieces when you glue them together. If you measure carefully you'll even be able to hide the joints under the vertical partitions. Use a biscuit joint below the window openings to keep the vertical partitions lined up.

Need a small bookcase? No problem. You can make this bookcase smaller, too. You can even edge band both sides of the shelves and use the unit as a room divider. Just be sure to fasten it to the floor.

You can also make it low, with a piece of glass on the top for a contemporary sofa table. For a

low design, skip the trim screws in the top edge banding (parts B) and just glue it on. When it comes time to assemble, epoxy the threaded rods into the square holes in the bottom of the top partitions. Then assemble and fasten the parts together, from the bottom, with regular hex nuts.

Rout, Drill and Assemble

Use your router to cut the grooves that house the hidden assembly and mounting hardware. Then counterbore for the nuts and washers, and drill the shelves for threaded rods. Assembly is a breeze—just slip the parts together and tighten the nuts.

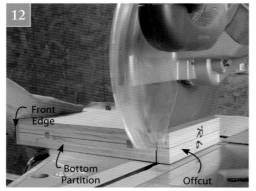

12

Front Edge · Bottom Partition · Offcut

Trim off ¾ in. of the back edge of the bottom partitions (parts L6, M6 and R6). This provides clearance for your wall's baseboard so the bookcase stands flush against the wall. Make sure to re-label the backs of the bottom partitions (L6, M6 and R6) with their location markings.

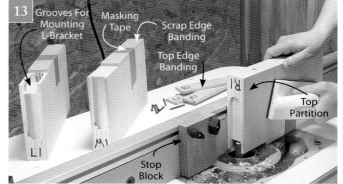

13

Grooves For Mounting L-Bracket · Masking Tape · Scrap Edge Banding · Top Edge Banding · Top Partition · Stop Block

Rout the grooves for the wall-mounting brackets into the top partitions (parts L1, M1 and R1, see Fig. E for details). First remove the top edge banding strips (parts B) and replace them with short pieces of scrap edge banding. These temporary pieces are needed as spacers because the front edge banding overhangs the top edge. They are left short so they don't interfere when routing the groove. Use a 1-in.-diameter straight bit for the routing. Cut the deeper top groove in two or three passes.

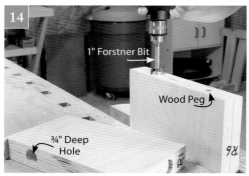

14

1" Forstner Bit · Wood Peg · ¾" Deep Hole

Drill holes for the assembly nuts and washers. Drill into the center of the square wood pegs that are glued into the panels. Only the top and bottom partitions (parts L, M and R) receive these large holes.

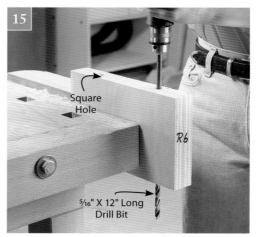

15

Square Hole · R6 · ⁵⁄₁₆" X 12" Long Drill Bit

Ream out the square holes in all of the vertical partitions (parts L, M and R) with a long drill bit. This removes any dried glue, wood splinters and remaining wood pegs.

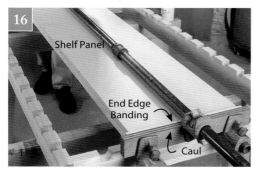

16

Shelf Panel · End Edge Banding · Caul

Edge band the shelves (parts A). Start with the ends (parts E) and then add the front edge banding (parts F). Trim any overhanging edge banding with a handsaw and flush trim the long edges with a flush-trim bit in your router.

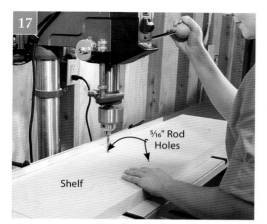

Drill holes for the threaded rods in the shelves. Lay out these holes carefully and use a drill press to ensure that the holes go straight through the shelves. See Fig. D for the layout dimensions. After all the parts for the bookcase are fabricated, do a final sanding. Then apply a clear finish of your choice. Finishing prior to final assembly is a lot easier than brushing or spraying all those inside corners once the bookcase is put together.

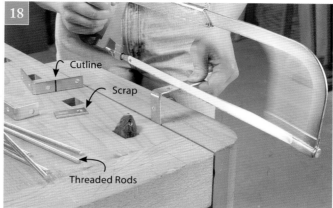

Saw the mounting L-bracket and threaded rods to length. The length of the short leg on the mounting angle is not critical, just cut it off about ¼-in. beyond the first hole.

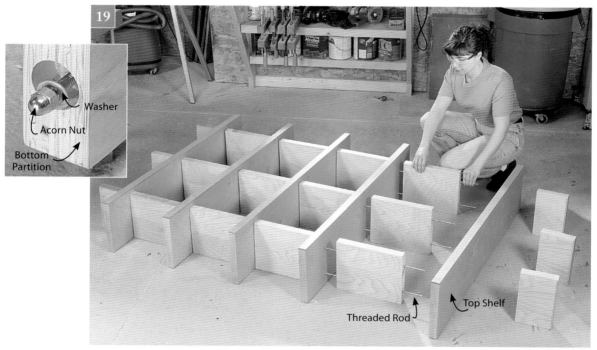

Assemble the prefinished bookcase on the floor. Lay the parts on their backs and slide them onto the threaded rods. Start with the bottom partitions and shelves and work your way to the top. The acorn nut at the bottom acts as a bolt head and makes tightening a lot easier. After sliding all the parts together, put a regular hex nut and washer on the top end. Lightly tighten the parts using a socket wrench at each end. The vertical partitions should self-align, but if you notice one that's slightly out of alignment, give it a little bump until it's lined up. When everything is perfectly aligned, do a final tightening.

Anchor It to the Wall

It's important to anchor this bookcase (like all tall bookcases) to the wall. Bookcases tend to be unstable, and adding books and such can make the situation even worse. Once an unanchored bookcase starts to fall, there's little stopping it. *Always* anchor bookcases and other tall furniture to the wall, especially if small children are around.

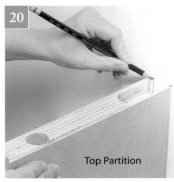

Mark the inside of the groove on the wall after standing the bookcase against it.

Brackets hold the bookcase to the wall and are totally hidden.

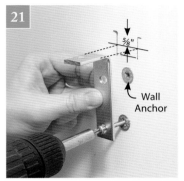

Attach the L- brackets to the wall with screws and wall anchors. Align the top of the L-bracket ⅝-in. down from the top of the pencil marks.

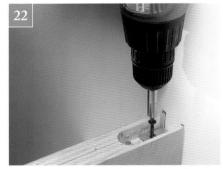

Screw the L-bracket to the bookcase. If you're setting your bookcase on carpet you should leave the screw head sticking up about ¼-in. above the L-bracket. This allows the bookcase to settle into the carpet. Once you've secured the L-brackets to the bookcase you can screw the top edge banding strips (parts B) back in place.

Cutting List
Overall dimension 48" wide x 67¼" tall x 11" deep

Part	Name	Qty.	Dimensions TxWxL	Material
A	Shelf parts	10	¾" x 10¾" x 47½"	Birch Plywood
B	Top edge banding for top partitions	3	¼" x 1½" x 9¾"	Birch
C	Front edge banding for top and bottom partitions	6	¼" x 1½" x 6"	Birch
D	Front edge banding for center partitions	12	¼" x 1½" x 12"	Birch
E	End edge banding for shelves	10	¼" x 1½" x 10¾"	Birch
F	Front edge banding for shelves	5	¼" x 1½" x 48"	Birch
L1,M1,R1	Top partition parts	6	¾" x 9¾" x 5¾"	Birch Plywood
L,M,R, 2-5	Center partition parts	24	¾" x 9¾" x 12"	Birch Plywood
L6,M6,R6	Bottom partition parts	6	¾" x 9" x 6"	Birch Plywood
Hardware				
	¼ -20 threaded rod	6	66¼" long	
	Hex nuts	6	¼-20	
	Acorn nuts	6	¼-20	
	Flat washers	12	For ¼" rod	
	Metal L-brackets	3	¾" x 3"	
	Wall anchors	6		

by JOHN NESSET

Free-Form Wall Shelves

VERSATILE, CREATIVE AND UNIQUE

Here's a versatile shelf that allows for a creative, one-of-a-kind edge treatment. Hung on the wall without any visible means of support, these shelves are real eye catchers.

Choose boards at least 1¼-in. thick and no more than about 7-in. wide. Wood with wane, bark pockets or end checks is a perfect candidate. (This is a great way to use reject boards that are too pretty to throw away or burn.)

First, true up the top and back edge with a hand plane or jointer. The board's back edge is planed a degree or two less than perpendicular to keep objects from rolling off of the shelf. Next, position keyhole hangers out toward the shelves ends. Space the hangers every 16-in. so the shelves can be mounted directly to wall studs. Mount keyholes either horizontally or vertically and place near the top edge to provide a bearing surface below the attachment point. Mark the hangers' profile with a sharp knife and carefully chisel out the mortises to the exact depth of the hangers. Drill a recess

at the bottom of each mortise (approx. ⁵⁄₁₆-in. deep) to allow the wall-mounted screws to securely engage the hangers.

Shape the rest of the shelf. Cut the gently curved and beveled ends on a bandsaw. Don't think too hard about how each piece should look. I've had good results letting the grain figure determine the shelf's shape. Remove the loose or broken stuff and smooth out any rough edges with a carver's gouge.

Finish with a couple of coats of oil, hang it up and you've got a conversation piece that will wow your houseguests.

Figure A: Wall Mount

2" x #10 Pan Head Screw

2" x 4" Wall Stud

½" Drywall

92 Degrees

by LUKE HARTLE

Dovetailed Bookcase

NO SCREWS, NO NAILS—TAPERED SLIDING DOVETAILS HOLD IT ALL TOGETHER

S imple, beautiful, strong. This bookcase is just six boards held together using one elegant joint: the tapered sliding dovetail. Dovetails join the shelves to the sides and the sides to the top. This joint has a well-deserved reputation for being fussy to cut and fit, but I've devised two jigs so easy to use that you can't go wrong.

I used 1⅛-in.-thick wood for this bookcase because it makes the piece look strong and substantial. However, using my jigs, you can make the bookcase from ⅞-in. boards. I built my bookcase from hard maple. It doesn't have a dominant grain pattern, like red oak, so the exposed dovetails are easy to see. They look terrific!

Prepare the Stock

Glue up and mill the shelves (A), sides (B) and top (C) to final width and length (Fig. A, Photo 1). All of the pieces are equal to or less than 12 in. wide, so you can run them through a planer to even up the joints. To succeed with the dovetail joinery, it's essential that all these parts are dead flat. Use a crosscut sled to ensure the ends are square.

Rout the Tails

Use a shop-made dovetail jig to make perfectly tapered dovetails on the shelves and sides (Photo 2; Fig. B). Note that a joint's wide end goes on the *front* of a shelf but on the *back* of the side (Fig. A). The shelves slide in from the front, so the exposed dovetails are the wide end.

The top slides in from the front because the joint is stopped. Rout both ends of each shelf and the top end of each side.

Rout the Side Sockets

Lay the two sides together, like an open book, and mark the centerlines of the shelf sockets (Fig. A). Align the socket jig with these marks and rout all six (Photo 3).

Cut the shelves, sides and top to length using a crosscut sled. The ends must be absolutely straight and square to make tight-fitting dovetail joints. Clamp a long stop arm to the sled to ensure similar pieces are cut to the same length.

Stop Arm

Rout tapered dovetails on the ends of the shelves and sides. I've devised a shop-made jig that makes this complicated joint virtually foolproof.

Shelf

Tail Jig

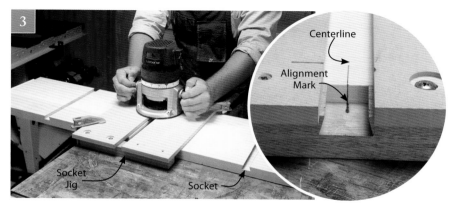

Socket Jig

Socket

Centerline

Alignment Mark

Rout sockets in the sides. This jig has a tapered opening that exactly mirrors the dovetail's taper. Line up the jig's alignment mark with each shelf's centerline (see inset).

Cutting List

Overall Dimensions: 42"H x 42"W x 12"D

Part	Name	Qty.	Dimensions (Th x W x L)
A	Shelf	3	1⅛" x 11" x 34¾"
B	Side	2	1⅛" x 11" x 41⅜"
C	Top	1	1⅛" x 12" x 42"

PROJECT REQUIREMENTS AT A GLANCE

Materials:

- 30 bd. ft. of 5/4 (1¼-in.) hard maple

Cost: $160

Tools:

- Planer
- Tablesaw
- Jointer
- Router

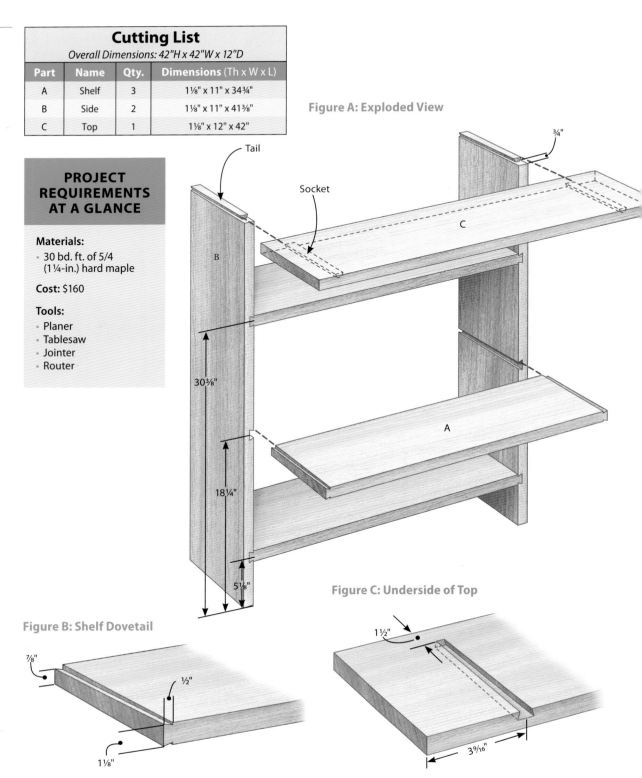

Figure A: Exploded View

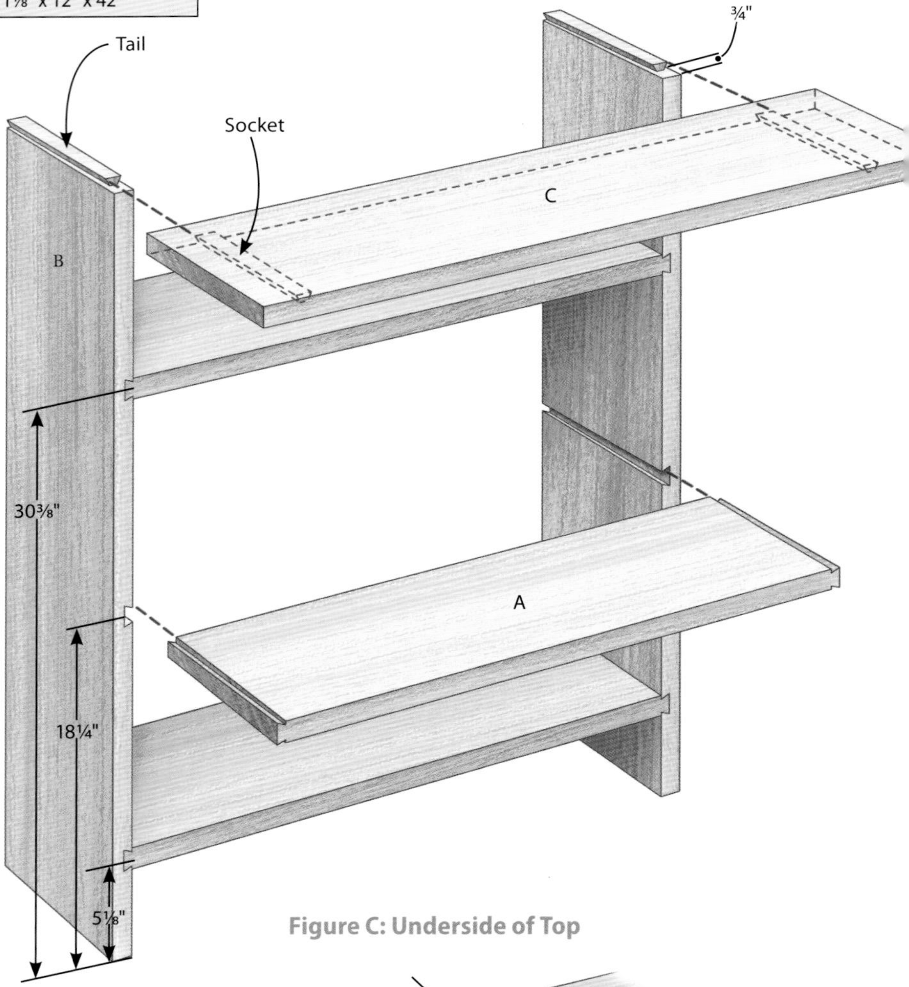
¾"
Tail
Socket
B
C
A
30⅜"
18¼"
5⅛"

Figure B: Shelf Dovetail

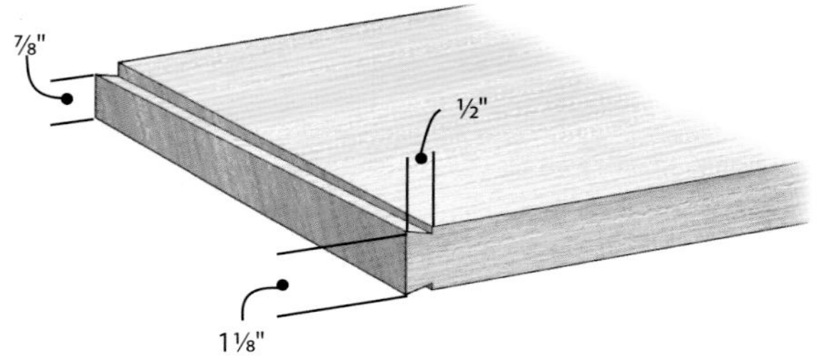
⅞"
½"
1⅛"

Figure C: Underside of Top

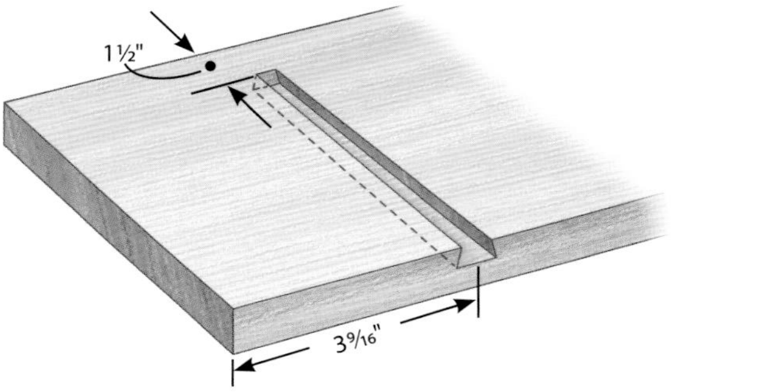
1½"
3⁹⁄₁₆"

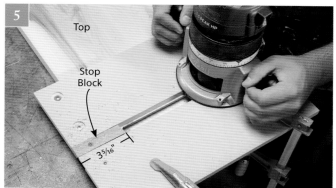

Assemble the shelves and sides. Glue all three shelves to one side; then add the other side before the glue sets. Tapered sliding dovetails don't become tight until they're almost home, so you can work at a comfortable pace.

Rout stopped sockets in the top. Place a block in the jig to stop the cut. These sockets don't go all the way across, because the top's front overhangs the sides. Here, the dovetail joint is "blind," or hidden.

Trim the front end of each side's dovetail. This is much easier to do with a handsaw than by machine. The shoulder you create will sit under the uncut portion of the top's socket.

Assemble the Case

Sand the shelves and sides; then glue them together (Photo 4). Apply a thin layer of glue to either the socket or the dovetail—it's not necessary to spread glue on both parts. It's easy to slide the joint most of the way home by hand, but keep a mallet or pipe clamp handy for the final push.

Rout the Top Sockets

Be fussy when laying out the sockets in the top, because there's little or no room for error. Mark the center of the top dovetails on the sides. Turn the glued case upside down and place it on the top. Transfer the centerlines of the dovetails to the top (Fig. C). Line up the socket jig on these marks (Photo 5). Note that the jig's narrow side faces the top's front.

Add the Top

Trim the side's dovetails (Photo 6, Fig. A). Sand the top and glue it on (Photo 7). Round over all the edges of the top, sides and shelves with sandpaper.

Slide the top into place. Dovetail joinery makes this bookcase extremely rigid, even without a back panel. You can load it with heavy books and never worry about it sagging or falling apart.

by DAVID RADTKE

Cottage Bookcase

RECLAIMED DOUGLAS FIR GIVES RUSTIC CHARM

Every board of this bookcase is full of character—nail holes, gouges and even hammer marks. That's because each piece was pulled from an old Montgomery Ward warehouse in Baltimore.

Originally part of a large shelving system built more than 75 years ago, our reclaimed boards still retained a dusty aroma and had mellowed to a rich warm color. These unique characteristics influenced the design of our bookcase—straightforward and reminiscent of rustic folk furniture. The bookcase is

Montgomery Ward warehouse, Baltimore, Maryland, 1925

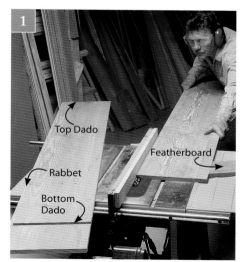

Cut ⅜-in.-deep rabbets and dadoes into the side panels to accept the solid wood back pieces as well as the top and bottom panels. Use a featherboard to keep the panel tight to the fence to ensure an even edge on the rabbets. The bottom horizontal panel should fit snugly into the dado, so adjust your dado blade precisely or make multiple passes.

Bore evenly spaced 1-in. holes for the shelf supports. Mount a board onto the table of your drill press and attach a fence to it for exact centering of each hole. Once the holes are drilled, cut each piece to length, then rip it down the middle to make a matched pair for each side. Glue and clamp each pair to the inside edge of each side panel.

constructed from ¾-in. boards. Unlike most plywood-backed bookcases, the back of this bookcase is assembled from individual pieces splined together.

To build this piece you'll need a tablesaw, a jointer, a router and a biscuit joiner, although you could use a doweling jig. A large assembly table or a make-shift work surface made from a ¾-in. plywood sheet laid over sawhorses is a must. Figure on spending about three days in your shop to complete this piece.

Working with Reclaimed Fir

Because the surface of the boards was in pretty rough shape, each ¾-in.-thick piece was first surfaced to ¹¹⁄₁₆ in. To keep everything simple, the dimensions

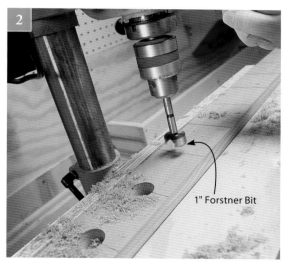

Screw the top into the upper dadoes of the sides and glue and clamp the bottom into the lower dadoes. Measure the diagonals. They must be equal to square the case. Once the glue is dry, flip the case face down. Make sure the case is square and screw blocks along the sides and top into the work surface to keep it square as you install the back panels.

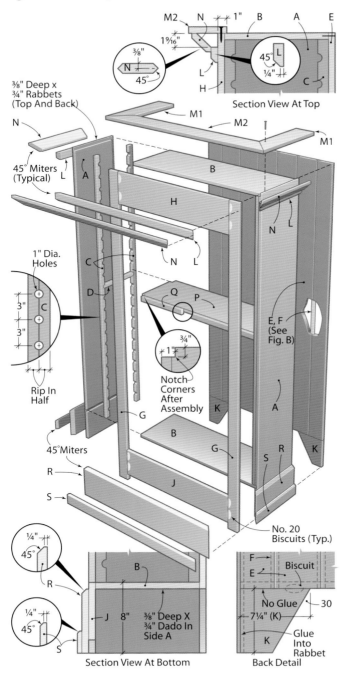

Figure A: Assembly

M2   N   1"   B   A   E

1⁹⁄₁₆"

3⁄8"

N

45°

45°   L

1⁄4"

L

H

C

Section View At Top

3⁄8" Deep x
3⁄4" Rabbets
(Top And Back)

M1

N

M2

M1

45° Miters
(Typical)   L

A

B

H

N   L

1" Dia.
Holes

C

3"

C

3"

D

N   L

E, F
(See
Fig. B)

Rip In
Half

Q   P

3⁄4"

1"

Notch
Corners
After
Assembly

K

A

G

B

G

S   R   K

45° Miters

R

S

J

No. 20
Biscuits (Typ.)

1⁄4"

45°

R

1⁄4"

45°

S

B

J   8"   3⁄8" Deep X
3⁄4" Dado In
Side A

Section View At Bottom

F

E

Biscuit

No Glue

7¼" (K)

30

Glue
Into
Rabbet

K

Back Detail

in the illustrations and the Cutting List assume ¾-in.-thick material.

When you buy reclaimed wood, keep in mind you may not be able to get all the lengths or widths you'd like. Be sure to specify longer pieces to make the sides and face frame. Shorter pieces can be made into shelves and moldings. Order about 30 percent extra to make up for a lot of end cuts and just plain bad stuff (too much character!). Because you'll be making wide panels, choose pieces that are cup free. Nearly all the wood I picked up was flat, dry and after that many years, well seasoned.

Douglas fir splinters easily, and even more so when it's as old and dry as this stuff. Keep a tweezers handy.

Preparing the Case Sides

After matching the grain (the sides (A) are the most critical) be sure to joint the edges for a straight and square edge glue-up. Make the panels a bit wider than needed, then rip them to exact width on your tablesaw. Next cut the dadoes (Photo 1) in the top of the sides. Now cut another dado 8-in. up from the bottom of each inner side panel. Finish the grooving process with rabbet cuts along the whole length on the inside backs of each panel.

Making the Vertical Shelf Standards

Rip two pieces 2½-in. wide from your stock to make parts C. Keep them longer than needed and trim to length later. Mark them every 3 in. (Photo 2) with a square. Set up a fence and a plywood base attached to your drill press table. Set the fence so the 1-in.

Forstner bit will drill holes in the center of the piece. After drilling the length of holes for each standard, cut them to length. Leave equal distance from the holes on the top and bottom ends. Mark the tops.

Rip each piece in half on your tablesaw. Finish sand these pieces, then glue and clamp them to the cabinet sides, as shown in Fig. A. Don't cut the horizontal shelf supports (D) yet.

Assembling the Case

Lay out the side panels (A) and the top and bottom panels (B) on a large flat work space. Apply glue to the dadoes and ends of the bottom panel. Clamp this lower assembly face up (Photo 3) and make sure the top and bottom panels are flush with the front edges of the sides. Screw the sides to the top panel (they'll be hidden by the cornice). Before the glue sets, make sure the case is square.

Making and Installing the Back

Rip your back pieces to 5 in. Make sure they're good and straight. Install a ¼-in. rabbeting (slot cutting) bit with a ⅜-in. depth of cut. Make a simple jig like the one shown in Photo 4 to hold the pieces flat to your workbench. Cut the slots in the center of the edge moving from right to left to avoid tear out. A couple passes should do the trick. Finish routing each slot with a left to right pass to make sure the bit has cut its full depth. Flip the piece end for end and rout the other edge. Mark the front and back of each piece.

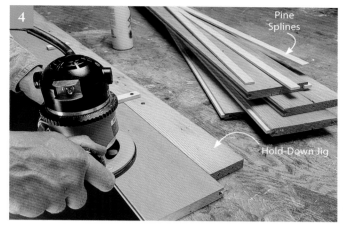

Rip, then joint the edges of all the back pieces. Rout a ¼-in. groove into the center of each side edge. Glue a slightly thinner than ¼-in. by ¹¹⁄₁₆-in. pine spline into one side of each back piece. Once the glue has dried, fit each back piece to the back of the case. Start in the center and work your way to the sides.

Glue the face frame to the front edges of the case. Be sure it's perfectly aligned, then clamp it to the case every foot along the perimeter. Trim the slight over-hang on each side with a block plane once the glue is dry.

¼" Slotting Bit

Shape the cornice moldings on the tablesaw. Set the blade at 45 degrees. Run each board through on both faces to create bevel edges, then repeat for the other edge. The other narrow cornice molding is a simple 45-degree piece cut from a 1¾-in. piece of ¾-in. stock.

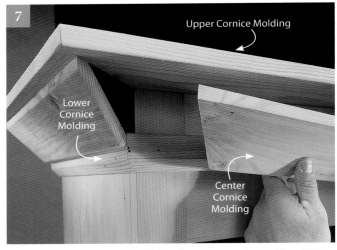

Fit the center cornice molding (N) to the upper cornice molding (M1) and to the lower cornice molding (L). See Fig. A for exact dimensions.

From new pine boards, rip the splines (F) a hair thinner than the slots. Don't use the fir to make the splines because it may split and new pine will be more forgiving during assembly. Glue the splines into the slot on one side only. Leave the spline out of the last board (Fig. B) because you'll need to rip it to width later. Let the glue dry.

Now flip the case over so the back faces up. Screw some blocks into the workbench tightly against the case after rechecking it for square. The blocks keep the case from shifting out of square as you nail the back pieces to the top and bottom panels. Make sure the back pieces are cut to length.

Don't glue the three center panels together—just nail them in place with #4 common nails leaving 3⁄32-in. space between the edges so you can see the splines. Now measure for the remaining pieces. Rip the outer two pieces. Glue the splines of the two outer panels, as shown in Fig. B (maintain the 3⁄32-in. spacing). Fit them in place, then glue and nail each outer pair of panels to the case sides. Biscuit and glue the diagonal corner brace (K), as shown in Fig. A.

Making and Installing the Face Frame

Rip the stiles for the face frame from wide stock. Choose pieces with similar grain. Cut the wider horizontal rail pieces about 1⁄16-in. longer than the width of the case (minus the stiles) so you'll have a bit extra to trim after the face frame is glued to the case.

Now align the edges of the rails with the stiles and mark your biscuit locations (or use a doweling jig). Glue and clamp the

Figure B: Back Detail

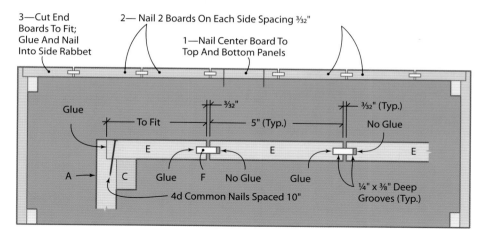

3—Cut End Boards To Fit; Glue And Nail Into Side Rabbet

2— Nail 2 Boards On Each Side Spacing ³⁄₃₂"

1—Nail Center Board To Top And Bottom Panels

Glue

³⁄₃₂"

³⁄₃₂" (Typ.)

To Fit

5" (Typ.)

No Glue

E

E

E

A

C

Glue

F

No Glue

Glue

¼" x ³⁄₈" Deep Grooves (Typ.)

4d Common Nails Spaced 10"

assembly, check the diagonal measurements and square it. Set the assembly aside to dry.

Finish sand the face frame and glue and clamp it to the front edge of the case (Photo 5).

Making and Installing the Moldings

Cutting the profiles of these moldings is simple. The lower cornice molding (L) is cut from a 1¾ in. wide by ¾ in. thick board. Set the tablesaw blade at a 45-degree angle. Set the fence so you'll leave a ¼-in. flat section at the bottom of the molding, as shown in Fig. A. Use a similar technique to make the base moldings R and S. Notice that the lower base molding is first resawn to a ½-in. thickness.

To make the wider center cornice molding (N), rip a 6-ft. long piece at about 3¼ in., as shown in Photo 6. Then set the tablesaw blade at 45 degrees and the fence at 3 in. from the middle of the cut (⅜ in.

up from the table surface). Now make a 45-degree rip on all four sides of the piece. Finish sand all molding edges.

Install the cornice and base moldings as shown in Photo 7 and Fig. A. Do not glue these pieces to the case. The sides of the bookcase will move with seasonal humidity changes and because the grain direction of the side moldings is running opposite, any glue joints here will fail. It's okay to use nails here because the wood is full of distress marks and any additional holes won't be noticed. Nails will adjust themselves in the moldings to counteract any wood movement. If you don't want to use nails, you can use screws from the inside of the bookcase, but you'll have to drill elongated screw holes to allow for wood movement.

Finishing Touches

The shelf supports mentioned earlier are cut from ¾ in. stock to a 1-in. width. Cut them ⅛ in. longer and belt sand a rounded edge on each end to fit into the shelf support. A little trial and error works best. Work for a snug fit.

Glue up and clamp boards to make the shelf blanks (P). Next glue the nosings (Q) to the shelves. The nosings add extra stiffness to the shelf as well as a heftier appearance. Finish sand the shelves once the glue is dry and notch them to fit around the shelf supports.

Sand the entire bookcase with 150-grit sandpaper followed by 220-grit. Clean away the dust with a tack rag before finishing.

Because of the beautiful natural patina of the wood, I simply used a clear wax finish. I avoided oil because the oil would darken and make this softwood blotchy. The wax gives a clean, even look and a sealer isn't necessary. Rub the first coat on with a cloth, let it sit for 10 minutes, then buff it out and repeat the same process the next day. The wax gives the wood a very light sheen. Colored waxes are also available if you want a deeper color tone on your piece.

Cutting List

Overall dimensions: 76¾" H x 40¾" W x 16⅜" D

Part	Name	Qty.	Dimensions
A	side panels	2	¾" x 12¼" x 76"
B	top and bottom panels	2	¾" x 11½" x 33¼"
C	shelf standards (rip into pairs)	2	¾" x 2½" x 67¼"
D	shelf supports	10	¾" x 1" x 10"
E	case back panels (rip outer pair to fit)	7	¾" x 5" x 68¾"
F	pine splines	6	⁷⁄₆₄" x ¹¹⁄₁₆" x 68¾"
G	face frame stiles	2	¾" x 2½" x 76"
H	upper face frame rail	1	¾" x 7¼" x 29"
J	lower face frame rail	1	¾" x 6½" x 29"
K	back corner braces	2	¾" x 7¼" x 7¼"
L	lower cornice molding*	1	¾" x 1¾" x 6'
M1	upper cornice moldings (sides)*	2	¾" x 4⅜" x 17"
M2	upper cornice molding (front)*	1	¾" x 4⅜" x 42"
N	center cornice molding*	1	¾" x 3¼" x 6'
P	shelves	5	¾" x 10⅜" x 32⁷⁄₁₆"
Q	shelf nosings	5	¾" x 1¼" x 32⁷⁄₁₆"
R	base molding (cut to fit)	1	¾" x 7¼" x 6'
S	lower base molding (cut to fit)	1	½" x 2½" x 6'

* cut to fit

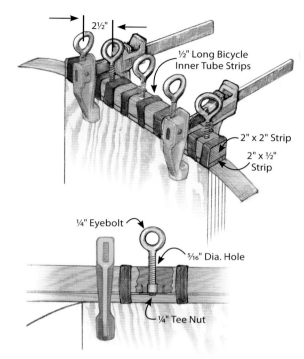

2½"

½" Long Bicycle
Inner Tube Strips

2" x 2" Strip

2" x ½"
Strip

¼" Eyebolt

5/16" Dia. Hole

¼" Tee Nut

Edge-Banding Clamp

I ran out of clamps and patience the last time I applied a veneered edge to a long piece of plywood. The tangle of clamps to hold the veneer and cauls in place was more than I could take! To make life simpler, I came up with a slick way to clamp edge banding onto the ends of long boards without the need for long, cumbersome pipe clamps.

Now I glue my edge banding material onto the board's end and place my jig over it. Then I add a few clamps over the jig to hold it in place. A few twists of the eye bolts pushes the lower strip toward the edge banding material.

James Mattea
Milwaukee, WI

Router Dado Jig

In the course of my work as a contractor, I often need to build cabinets and bookshelves on site—without the luxury of shop tools. I gave up on the flimsy router fence supplied with the machine and made the jig shown in the sketch. The router base now slides between two fixed-aluminum guides with no chance of slippage or accident. I used some salvaged track, but aluminum angle ought to work, as well. I attached the piece of 1-in. scrap at one end to square up the jig against the cabinet sides.

Anthony Roberts
Candler, NC

Aluminum
Track

Block to Square
Fixture to an Edge

by TOM CASPAR

Two-Part Bookcase

HERE'S A BIG BOOKCASE YOU CAN BUILD IN A SMALL SHOP

Building a tall bookcase can stretch the limits of a small shop. We all know that big boards can be a bear to handle and glue up, so I've taken an old Scandinavian design and sliced it up into bite-size pieces. My solution is to break the bookcase into two interlocking sections that require only short and narrow stuff. Not to mention, that's the only way I could get it out of my shop and up the basement stairs!

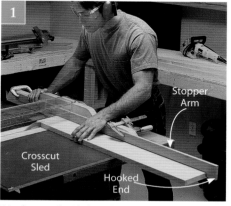

Stopper Arm

Crosscut Sled

Hooked End

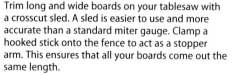

Trim long and wide boards on your tablesaw with a crosscut sled. A sled is easier to use and more accurate than a standard miter gauge. Clamp a hooked stick onto the fence to act as a stopper arm. This ensures that all your boards come out the same length.

Side View of Bookcase

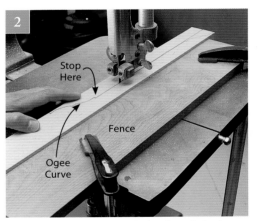

Rip the stepped board (C) on the bandsaw. A simple fence helps you make a straight cut. Stop the cut at the top of the ogee curve and withdraw the board. Remove the fence and cut out the ogee.

Glue the upper case sides from 1-in.-thick rough boards that are planed to ⅞-in. thick. This leaves some untouched low spots, but that's ok. Align the outside boards so their bottoms are even.

Biscuits join the shelves and sides. It's a snap to put together wide boards at right angles with a plate joiner. But biscuits alone aren't enough to make a stiff case, so I've added backboards that lock the whole bookcase into a rigid unit.

Materials and Tools

Rather than splurge on the best quality lumber simply to make shelves, you can save money on this project by using a lower grade of hardwood, No. 1 Common. You'll find many good boards that are too short or narrow to make the best grade but are perfect for this bookcase. I used No. 1 Common birch because it's inexpensive, a light color (the case looks less massive) and stiff enough to support heavy books. You'll need about 75 bd. ft.

As an alternative you can use ¾-in.-thick boards from a home center. Pick straight ones, glue them together and plane them to ⅝ in. I built a prototype bookcase this way and it worked just fine. To tell the truth,

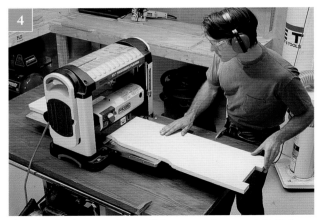

Plane the glued-up case sides until there are no low spots left. All the parts of this bookcase should be the same thickness, which can be anywhere from ¾ in. to a minimum of ⅝ in.

Do you have a portable planer?

Great, because we've kept every part less than 12-in. wide. That means you can flatten the sides and shelves with your planer.

Do you buy lumber at a home center?

Go ahead and buy pre-thicknessed ¾-in. boards. Our plans work fine with this time-saving wood or with No. 1 Common rough lumber.

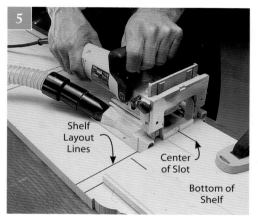

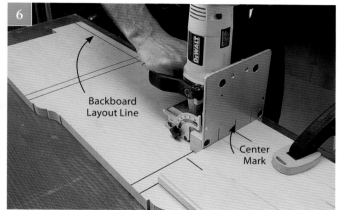

Cut biscuit slots in the ends of the shelves. You can't go wrong if you clamp each shelf in position, right above the double lines. Set the shelf in from the back edge by the thickness of one backboard.

Cut more biscuit slots in the case side. Stand the plate joiner up on end and butt it against the end of the shelf. Align the center mark on the bottom of the machine with the pencil mark on the bottom of the shelf.

I preferred its slim look to one made of thicker wood. However, I found that ⅝-in. thick shelves bend under a lot of weight, so they wouldn't be suitable for a set of encyclopedias.

You'll need the three basic machines for processing solid wood to make this bookcase from rough lumber: a tablesaw, a jointer and a planer. (If you build with pre-planed, ¾-in. boards that have one straight edge, you can get by without a jointer.) A crosscut sled for your tablesaw isn't required but it sure makes life easier. In addition, you'll need a router, plate joiner, bandsaw or jigsaw, an accurate framing square and eight pipe clamps to hold the case together during glue up.

Any white or yellow glue works fine for the biscuit joints, because both glues contain the water needed to swell the biscuits. Use a special yellow glue with a long open time if you're going to glue up the cases by yourself and don't like working like a speed demon!

Figure A: Biscuit Placement

#20 biscuits are plenty strong to hold a shelf's weight. They won't shear off under a load because the grain of a biscuit runs diagonally.

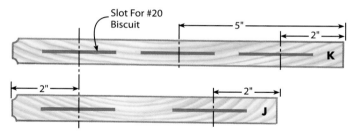

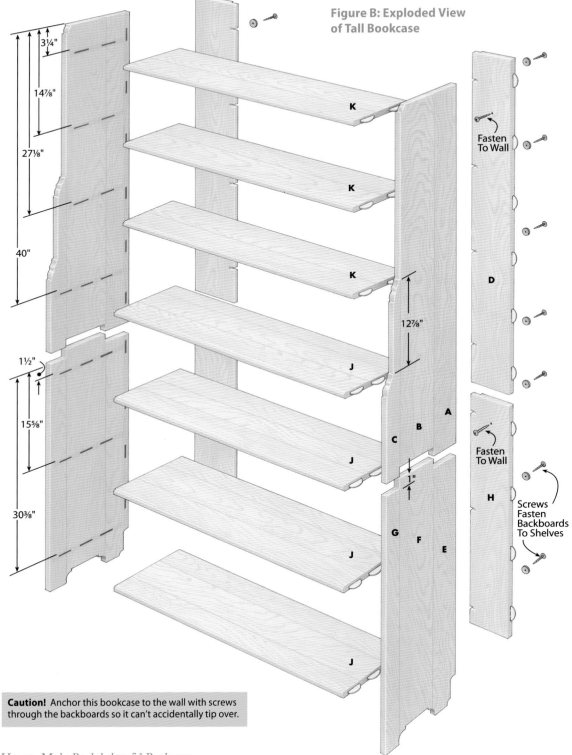

Figure B: Exploded View of Tall Bookcase

3¼"

14⅞"

27⅛"

40"

K

K

K

J

12⅞"

D

Fasten To Wall

1½"

15⅝"

30⅜"

J

J

J

J

C

B

A

G

F

E

1"

H

Fasten To Wall

Screws Fasten Backboards To Shelves

Caution! Anchor this bookcase to the wall with screws through the backboards so it can't accidentally tip over.

Figure C: Detail of Top Cutout

It's easier to cut this with a jigsaw than a bandsaw because it's hard to balance the board on a bandsaw's table.

Figure D: Details of Ogee Curve and Shelf Molding

This is a 50-percent reduction. Make a copy, double its size on a photocopy machine, paste it onto an index card and cut it out.

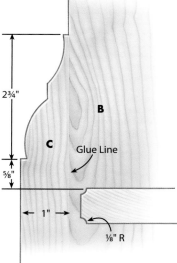

Figure E: Detail of Bottom Cutout

Scribe the back of your bookcase to fit around your baseboard molding. The back of the bookcase should fit tight against the wall so the bookcase can be firmly anchored.

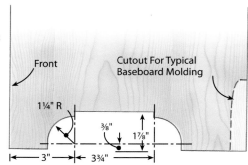

Figure F: Connection Between Top and Bottom

The top half of the bookcase fits snugly onto the bottom half. The lower backboards (H) prevent the top half from shifting side-to-side, and the notched sides lock in the top, front-to-back.

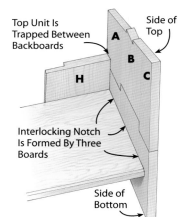

Figure G: Detail of Shelf Slots

Screwing the backboards to the shelves stiffens the bookcase, but an allowance must be made for the backboards to shrink and swell in width with the seasons. That's why the screw passes through a slot rather than a hole. The backboard is dadoed so the head of the screw doesn't stick out.

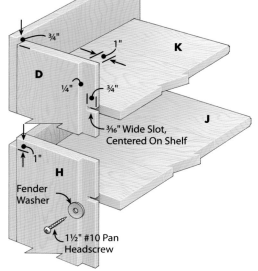

Cutting List
Overall Dimensions: 88" H X 36" W X 11" D

Part	Name	Qty.	Dimensions	Comments
Upper Unit				Glue together, thickness to ¾" and trim bottom end so overall length is 52."
A	Rear Board	2	⅞" x 3½" x 52¼"	
B	Middle Board	2	⅞" x 5½" x 51"	
C	Front Board	2	⅞" x 2" x 28½"	
D	Back	2	¾" x 5½" x 50"	
Lower Unit				Glue together, thickness to ¾" and trim middle board to fit notch in upper unit.
E	Rear Board	2	⅞" x 3½" x 36"	
F	Middle Board	2	⅞" x 5½" x 37¼"	
G	Front Board	2	⅞" x 2" x 36"	
H	Back	2	¾" x 5½" x 32½"	
Shelves				Glue up from ⅞" boards, thickness to ¾" and trim to length.
J	Wide Shelves	4	¾" x 10" x 34½"	
K	Narrow Shelves	3	¾" x 8" x 34½"	

Preparing Rough Lumber

For the sides and backboards, select untwisted boards. Rough cut your boards 1 in. over final length and ¼ in. over final width. Set your jointer to remove ⅟₃₂ in. Run one face over the jointer only a couple of times.

Run the other face of the boards through a portable planer until most rough spots are gone and the boards are all about ⅞-in. thick or a bit thinner. Joint one edge, rip the boards ⅟₃₂-in. over final width and joint the second edge. Pay attention to boards B and F—they must be exactly the same width.

Gluing the Sides

The upper and lower sides are composed of three boards that form a tongue and notch (Fig. F). There's no trick to getting the sides to nest together perfectly. It's simply a matter of being careful at glue up.

Start with the upper sides. Lay out the ogee curves on boards C and the cutouts on the top end of boards B (Figs. C and D). Cut out the curves on the bandsaw (Photo 2).

Dry clamp boards A, B and C together. Boards A and B are flush at the top. Boards A and C are flush at the bottom. Check both ends with a straightedge. Draw an alignment mark across all three boards (Photo 3).

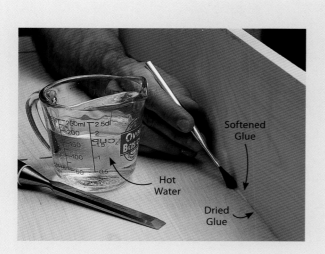

Hot Water

Softened Glue

Dried Glue

Oops!

Nuts! We forgot to remove some squeezed-out glue before it dried! Finish won't stick to it, so the glue has to be removed before we can move on. Fortunately, yellow glue can be softened with hot water and scraped off with a sharp chisel days after it has dried. Hot water turns the clear glue back to its original yellow color, so it's easy to see what must be removed. After scraping, wash the area with a rag dampened with hot water, let the wood dry and sand off the raised grain.

Square one end and trim the boards to exact length using a crosscut sled and a stopper arm (Photo 1).

Glue the upper sides together. Getting a perfect alignment end-to-end drove me nuts until I adopted the method of rubbing the boards together first, before clamping. Glue the lower sides the same way. Here, all three boards are flush at the bottom.

Milling the Sides and Shelves

Plane both faces of the sides and back-boards so they're ¾-in. thick (Photo 4). Congratulations if you've removed all of the low spots, but don't hang your head if you haven't. You can plane all of the boards thinner, down to ⅝ in., if that's what it takes. Remove the mill marks by sanding with 100- and 120-grit paper.

Here's how to use the crosscut sled to trim the top and lower sides until they mate: First, saw off ¼ in. from the bottom of both upper sides. This guarantees the bottoms are square and straight, leaving a 1-in.-deep notch. Then trim the tongues of the lower sides until they fit the notches. Because the middle boards (B and F) are exactly the same width, everything should fit tight as a glove.

Finish the lower sides by sawing the cutout at the bottom (Fig. E). It's easier to use a jigsaw than be a hero and try to balance the board on the small table of a bandsaw. Make a pattern of your baseboard molding and cut out the back corner of the side so it will fit tight up against the wall.

Lay out the positions of the shelves on both the upper and lower sides (Fig. B). The shelves will be set in from the back of the sides by the thickness of the backboards. Draw this backboard layout line on the sides, too (Photo 6).

Glue up the shelves, thickness and sand them, then rout the molding on their front edges (Fig. D). Trim them to length with the crosscut sled. Finally, lay out center marks for the biscuits on the bottom faces.

Now for the easy joinery. Cut biscuit slots in the sides and shelves at the same time (Photos 5 and 6). Use a framing square to make sure the shelves are clamped in the right place.

Fitting the Backboards

If it weren't for the backboards, this bookcase wouldn't last a week. These hard-working boards help lock the upper and lower sections together, but more importantly they stiffen the case (Figs. F and G). Cut the backboards to length, place them in position on the case sides and lay out the slots for the screws (Fig. G). Cut the slots on the tablesaw. Stand the backboards on edge against a miter gauge and make two overlapping cuts with a standard saw blade. Then cut the dadoes for the screwheads.

Cut biscuit slots to join the backboards and case sides. These biscuits align the backboard flush with the side, but do not add strength. Glue the backboards to the sides (Photo 7).

Glue the backboard onto the case side. Make sure it's square along the entire length. Check opposite each clamp as you tighten it down. Shift the head of the clamp in or out to change the angle of the backboard.

Final Assembly

The backboards also help you square up the whole bookcase when you glue the sides and shelves together. Thank goodness! You can get into lots of trouble by gluing things out of square, but this system is slick. Dry clamp each shelf in place with the biscuits loose in the slots and mark the shelf's position on the backboard (Photo 8). Make the pencil lines very light because you won't be able to get into the corners with an eraser after the glue up. That's the one downside of this easy method.

Take your time and walk through a dry run of the glue up before you attempt the real thing (Photo 9). Here's the best way to do the glue up, alone, without going crazy:

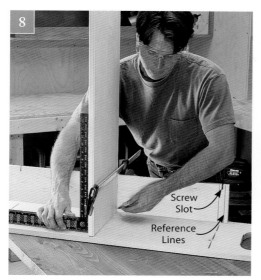

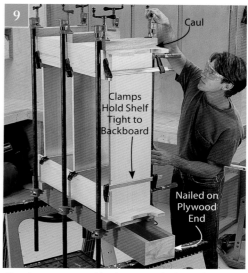

Mark the position of the shelves on the backboards with light pencil lines. These reference lines help you glue up the entire case square. Clamp each shelf in place, without glue, and adjust it until it's square to the case side.

Glue the upper case sides from 1-in.-thick rough boards that are planed to ⅞-in. thick. This leaves some untouched low spots, but that's ok. Align the outside boards so their bottoms are even.

Support one side with a narrow (7-in.), wooden box that leaves room for the clamp heads. Insert one shelf at a time, align it with the reference lines on the backboard and clamp it in place. Once all the shelves are upright, place the other case side on the ends of the shelves, clamp the shelves tight to the backboard and finally add the pipe clamps.

Finishing and Installation

After gluing both cases, sand them with 150-grit paper. Avoid dyeing or staining birch, because it has a tendency to unevenly soak up color and become blotchy. Even an oil finish can look bad, so stick with shellac, brushed-on varnish or lacquer.

This tall bookcase stands quite well on its own, but for safety, fasten it to the wall through the backboards. Then there'll be no chance for it to tip if a pet or rambunctious kid tries to climb the shelves!

by SETH KELLER

Sliding Door Bookcase

DUST-FREE DISPLAY AND NO HINGES TO MOUNT!

Glass doors make a bookcase, but doors that swing on hinges are a pain to install. Ditto for doors that lift open and slide back—on a Barrister's bookcase, for example. Regular sliding doors are much easier to install. In addition, they're ideal for a bookcase designed to fit in a space where swinging doors might get in the way.

This bookcase features super-smooth sliding door hardware that installs in minutes (see "Euro-Style Sliding Door Hardware," page 106). The shelves are generously deep and widely spaced. Following the lead of Arts and Crafts era builders, my design incorporates elements inspired by traditional Asian furniture.

Building this project requires two sheets of walnut plywood (one ¾-in. thick and one ¼-in. thick) and about 40 bd. ft. of ⁵⁄₄ walnut. The total cost, including glass and hardware, is about $600.

Caution! The blade guard must be removed for this operation.

Saw grooves for the sliding door tracks in the top and middle cabinet panels.

Rip both cabinet sides from a single wide panel in which all the dadoes have already been routed. This method guarantees that the dadoes in both sides will align.

Figure A: Exploded View

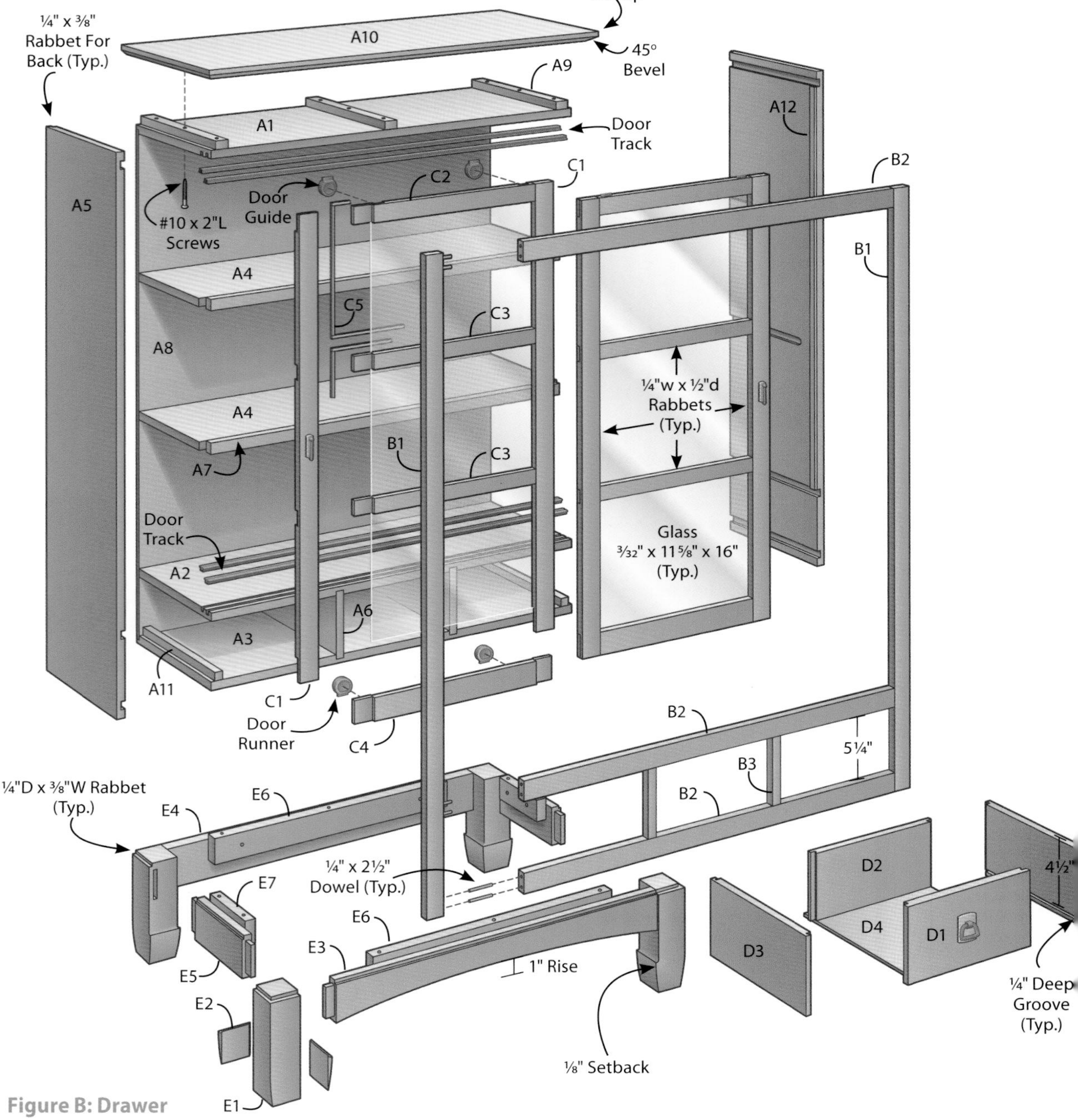
7/16" Lip
¼" x ⅜" Rabbet For Back (Typ.)
A10
45° Bevel
A9
A12
A1
Door Track
C1
B2
A5
Door Guide
C2
#10 x 2"L Screws
B1
A4
C5
C3
A8
¼"w x ½"d Rabbets (Typ.)
A4
B1
C3
A7
Door Track
Glass 3/32" x 11⅝" x 16" (Typ.)
A2
A6
A3
A11
C1
Door Runner
C4
B2
5¼"
B3
¼"D x ⅜"W Rabbet (Typ.)
E6
E4
B2
D2
4½"
¼" x 2½" Dowel (Typ.)
E7
E6
D4
D1
E3
D3
1" Rise
E5
¼" Deep Groove (Typ.)
E2
⅛" Setback
E1

Figure B: Drawer Divider Dadoes

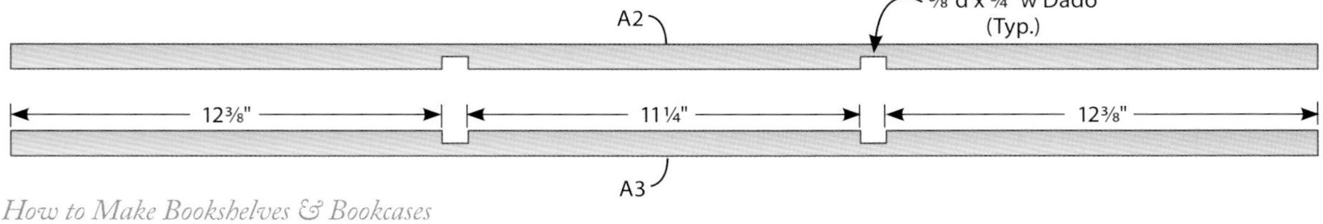
A2
⅜"d x ¾" w Dado (Typ.)
12⅜"
11¼"
12⅜"
A3

Build the Cabinet

1. Start by cutting the plywood panels and shelves to final size (Fig. A, A1-A4 and Cutting List).

2. Cut grooves for the sliding door tracks in the top and middle panels (Photo 1 and Fig. G). Cut the first groove in each panel, then reposition the fence and cut the second grooves).

3. Instead of cutting both cabinet sides (A5) to final size, cut one blank twice as wide as the sides, plus ⅛-in. Rip this blank in half after you've routed the dadoes, to create the sides (Photo 2). This method saves time and assures perfectly aligned dadoes. Plywood thickness is often undersize, so you may need a special bit to rout the dadoes (Fig. C).

4. Rout dadoes for the drawer dividers (A6) in the middle and bottom panels (Fig. B).

5. Rabbet the cabinet sides and the top and bottom panels for the ¼-in. plywood back.

6. Glue the cabinet sides and panels together (Photo 3). The top and bottom panels run the full depth of the cabinet. The middle panel aligns with the rabbet at the back. Use cauls to evenly distribute the clamping pressure.

7. Glue in the shelves. They slide in from the back. Make sure their back edges are flush with the rabbets for the cabinet's back.

8. Glue on the shelf edging (A7). The edging hides the stopped dadoes in the cabinet's sides.

Glue the cabinet together in stages, starting with the sides and the top, middle and bottom panels. Measure diagonally to be sure the cabinet is square. Glue in the shelves and drawer dividers later. This two-stage method doesn't require as many long clamps.

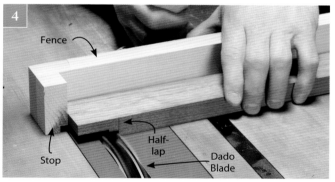

Outfit your miter gauge with a fence and a stop to cut the doors' half-lap joints. The stop guarantees that all the tenons will be the same length.

Assemble the doors in two steps. First glue and clamp the two middle rails to the stiles and check for squareness. Then add the top and bottom rails and recheck to make sure the assembly is square.

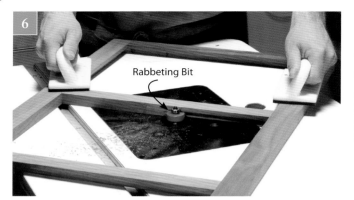

Rout rabbets for the glass in the back of each door. Make several shallow passes, rather than trying to rout full-depth in a single pass.

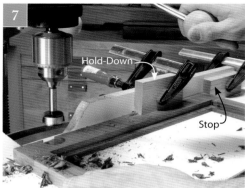

Bore holes into the doors for the sliding hardware. Use a fence and a stop for accurate positioning. Add a hold-down to keep the door flat on the table.

Use a drawer lock bit (right) to build the drawers. It creates both sides of the joint using the same setting. Rout the drawer fronts and backs flat on the table. Rout the sides vertically against the fence.

The protruding drawer bottoms act as stops by bumping the back of the cabinet. Install each drawer and measure how far it protrudes beyond the face frame. Trim that much from the drawer bottom's back edge to make the drawer flush.

9. Glue in the drawer dividers.

10. Fit and install the sliding door track.

11. Cut and fit the plywood back (A8), but don't install it.

12. Glue spacers (A9) on the top panel. They allow fastening the top.

13. Glue up the top (A10) and cut it to final length and width. Then rout a 45-degree bevel around the front and sides.

Install the Face Frame

14. Cut the face frame stiles and rails (B1 and B2) to final length and width.

15. Assemble stiles and rails with dowels. Make sure assembly is square and the bottom and middle rails are spaced 5¼ in.

16. Glue the face frame to the cabinet. Make sure the top of the frame's bottom rail is flush with the top of the cabinet's bottom panel. Center the frame on the cabinet—it should slightly overhang on both sides.

Create the horsehoof feet by building up the two inside faces of each leg. Miter the corner joint between the two added pieces.

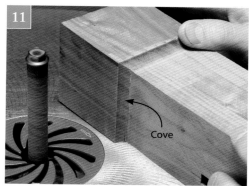

Sand coves to ease the transition between the glued-on blocks and the leg.

Bandsaw the outside curves on one face. Then turn the leg onto the adjacent face and cut a second set of curves.

Rout a rabbet on the top of the base. The rabbet creates a shadow line that hides slight dimensional differences between the cabinet and the base. Clamp on a support block to make the router ride smoothly and a ⅛-in. spacer to compensate for the apron's setback.

After the glue dries, trim the face frame stiles flush with the cabinet.

17. Glue on the dividers (B3).

18. Install the drawer guide blocks (A11). They fill the cavities behind the face frame, so the outside drawers track smoothly.

Build the Doors

19. Cut the door stiles and rails (C1-C4) to final width and length.

20. Cut the half-lap joints using a fence with a stop (Photo 4 and Fig. H). Make test cuts in scrap stock to dial in the blade's height and the stop's location.

21. Remove the stop to cut the stiles' inner half lap notches.

22. Dry fit each door to make sure all the joints fit. Glue and clamp the doors (Photo 5). Make sure the assembly is square.

23. Rout rabbets for glass in the backs of the doors (Photo 6). Square the corners with a chisel.

24. Drill holes for the sliding door hardware with a 35mm-dia. (or 1⅜-in.-dia.) Forstner bit (Photo 7 and Fig. D). The holes must be precisely centered 13 mm from the doors' edges. The depth of the

holes varies: The top holes are 12mm-deep; the bottom holes are 13mm-deep.

25. Press in sliding door hardware, install doors and test. The center stiles won't align when the doors are closed until you add the door stop (A12). Fine-tune alignment by adjusting the thickness of the stop or by jointing a smidge off one or more of the doors' outside edges.

Build the Drawers

26. Cut the drawer fronts, backs and sides (D1-D3) to final size. I made the grain flow across the front of the bookcase by cutting the drawer fronts sequentially from the same piece of walnut.

27. I use a router table and a special bit to cut the drawer joints (Photo 8).

28. Rout ¼-in.-deep grooves in the drawer fronts and sides for drawer bottoms (D4).

29. Glue the drawers together. Make sure the bottom edges of the drawer backs align with the tops of the grooves in the sides, so the bottoms will slide in.

30. Cut drawer bottoms to size, using leftover walnut plywood.

31. Insert drawer bottoms—they'll extend well beyond the back. Install each drawer to determine how much to trim to make drawer front flush with face frame (Photo 9). Remove bottom for trimming. Then reinstall and fasten with nails or screws.

Figure C: Cabinet Side Dadoes

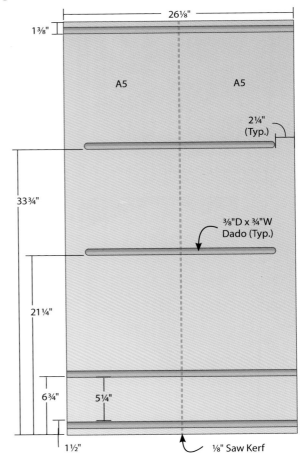

Build the Base

32. Glue together three 1-in.-thick pieces of walnut to create a blank for the legs (E1). Joint and plane this blank to 2¾-in.-square, then cut it into the four legs.

33. Cut mortises in the legs (Fig. F).

34. To create the Chinese-style horsehoof feet (Fig. E), rip and plane a pair of blocks (E2) to add to each leg.

35. Miter the blocks and glue them on (Photo 10).

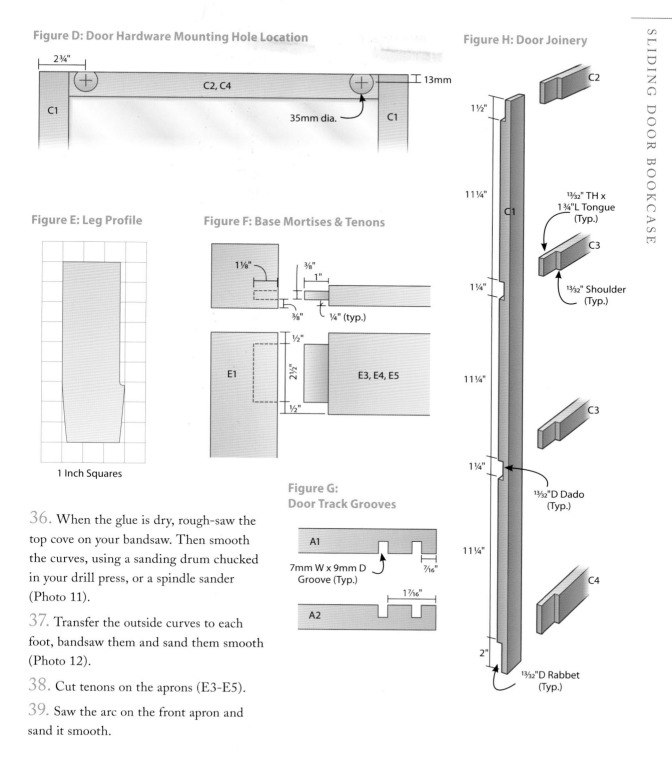

Figure D: Door Hardware Mounting Hole Location

2¾"

C2, C4

13mm

35mm dia.

C1

C1

Figure E: Leg Profile

1 Inch Squares

Figure F: Base Mortises & Tenons

1⅛"

⅜"

1"

⅜"

¼" (typ.)

½"

2½"

½"

E1

E3, E4, E5

**Figure G:
Door Track Grooves**

A1

7mm W x 9mm D
Groove (Typ.)

7/16"

A2

1 7/16"

Figure H: Door Joinery

C2

1½"

11¼"

C1

13/32" TH x
1¾"L Tongue
(Typ.)

C3

13/32" Shoulder
(Typ.)

1¼"

11¼"

C3

1¼"

13/32"D Dado
(Typ.)

11¼"

C4

2"

13/32"D Rabbet
(Typ.)

36. When the glue is dry, rough-saw the top cove on your bandsaw. Then smooth the curves, using a sanding drum chucked in your drill press, or a spindle sander (Photo 11).

37. Transfer the outside curves to each foot, bandsaw them and sand them smooth (Photo 12).

38. Cut tenons on the aprons (E3-E5).

39. Saw the arc on the front apron and sand it smooth.

40. Dry-fit the base and check its dimensions. The depth and width should match the cabinet. Glue the base together. Make sure it's square.

41. Rout a rabbet around the top of the base (Photo 13).

Final Assembly

42. Apply a finish before assembling the rest of the parts. I used a wipe-on urethane.

43. After the finish is dry, flip the cabinet upside down and align the base on the bottom of the cabinet.

44. Glue and screw cleats (E6 and E7) to bottom of cabinet (Photo 14). Attach base by screwing through the cleats into the aprons. Stand the cabinet right-side up.

45. From inside the cabinet, drill shank holes for screws through the top and the three spacers.

46. Clamp the top in position and then attach it with screws.

47. Screw on the plywood back (A8).

48. Install glass in the doors. Cut and fit the retaining strips (C5) and tack them in place.

49. Install hardware on the doors and drawers.

50. Install the doors. Engage the bottom hardware, then tip the door upright to engage the top (Photo 15). Remove the inner door's pull to install the outer door.

51. Load up the cabinet, then sit down and relax with a good book.

Attach the base to the cabinet with cleats. Glue and screw the cleats to the bottom of the cabinet, after positioning them flush against the aprons. Then screw the cleats to the aprons.

Install the inside door first, then the outside door. Installing both doors takes less than a minute.

Euro-Style Sliding Door Hardware

This system takes its cue from Euro-style cup hinges. The components press into 35-mm holes, install in seconds and adjust to fit. Each door requires two upper guides and two lower runners. Rollers integrated into the runners ride on the track's flange. The roller assembly adjusts in and out to raise or lower the door. Retractable tongues in the upper guides click up into the track after the door is tipped into position.

Cutting List

Overall dimensions: 14¾"D x 40¼"W x 58⅝"H

Part	Name	Materials	Qty.	Dimensions
Cabinet (w/out top)				**13¾" x 38¼" x 48¾"**
A1	Top Panel	Walnut Plywood	1	¾"** x 13" x 37½"
A2	Middle Panel	Walnut Plywood	1	¾"** x 12¾" x 37½"
A3	Bottom Panel	Walnut Plywood	1	¾"** x 13" x 37½"
A4	Shelf	Walnut Plywood	2	¾"** x 10" x 37½"
A5	Side*	Walnut Plywood	2	¾"** x 13" x 48¾"
A6	Drawer Divider	Walnut Plywood	2	¾"** x 6" x 12¾"
A7	Shelf Edging	Walnut	2	¾" x 1" x 36¾"
A8	Back	Walnut Plywood	1	¼"** x 37½" x 46⅝"
A9	Spacer	Pine	3	⅝" x 1¼" x 13"
A10	Top	Walnut	1	⅞" x 14¾" x 40¼"
A11	Drawer Guide Block	White Oak	2	¾" x ¾" x 12½"
A12	Door Stop	Walnut	1	¼" x ¾" x 39⅞"
Face Frame				**¾" x 38⅜"*** x 48¾"**
B1	Stile	Walnut	2	¾" x 1½" x 48¾"
B2	Rail	Walnut	3	¾" x 1½" x 35⅜"
B3	Divider	Walnut	2	¾" x ¾" x 5¼"
Door				**13⁄16" x 19⅛" x 39¾"**
C1	Stile	Walnut	4	13⁄16" x 1¾" x 39¾"
C2	Top Rail	Walnut	2	13⁄16" x 1½" x 19⅛"
C3	Middle Rail	Walnut	4	13⁄16" x 1¼" x 19⅛"
C4	Bottom Rail	Walnut	2	13⁄16" x 2" x 19⅛"
C5	Glass Retainer Strip	Walnut	24	3⁄16" x ⅜" x cut to length
Drawer			**3**	**5⅛" x 11³⁄16" x 13¼"**
D1	Front	Walnut	3	¾" x 5⅛" x 11³⁄16"
D2	Back	White Oak	3	½" x 4½" x 11³⁄16"
D3	Side	White Oak	6	½" x 5⅛" x 12¾"
D4	Bottom	Walnut Plywood	3	¼"** x 10⅝" x 13½"
Base				**9" x 13¾" x 38¼"**
E1	Leg	Walnut	4	2¾" x 2¾" x 9"
E2	Block	Walnut	8	¼" x 3" x 3"
E3	Front Apron	Walnut	1	⅞" x 3½" x 34¾"****
E4	Back Apron	Walnut	1	⅞" x 3½" x 34¾"****
E5	Side Apron	Walnut	2	⅞" x 3½" x 10¼"****
E6	Long Cleats	Pine	2	1" x 2½" x 24"
E7	Short Cleats	Pine	2	1" x 2" x 7¾"

*Rip both sides from one 26⅛"-wide blank   ***Trim flush after mounting
**Nominal plywood thickness   ****Includes 1"-long tenons on both ends

by RANDY JOHNSON

Display Cabinet

LOTS OF GLASS AND BUILT-IN LIGHTS SHOWCASE YOUR TREASURES

S ome cabinets are all about displaying the beauty of wood. This cabinet, with its glass doors, shelves and sides and built-in lighting, is all about displaying what's inside. Whether it's your collection of antique tools or fine porcelain, whatever you put inside is sure to shine.

Box Frames Make It Strong

The upper and lower box frames are the secret behind this cabinet's strength and rigidity (Fig. A). They join the two cabinet sides together and create a cabinet that is surprisingly strong and rigid. These are important attributes when building a tall cabinet with large glass doors because any flexing in the cabinet can cause the doors to go out of alignment.

Tools and Materials

The power tools you need to build this display cabinet include a tablesaw, jointer, planer, bandsaw (or jigsaw), and a router table and router. A mortising machine is helpful but you can also use

a drill and chisel to make the mortises. Other necessary tools include an electric drill, a plate joiner, a dado blade and a variety of router and drill bits.

Plan on using about 80 bd. ft. of 5/4 (1¼-in. thick) lumber for this project. If you use mahogany, the lumber will cost you about $400. Other hardwoods like rift-sawn oak, walnut, or ash would also work. Wood with straight grain works the best. Wavy-grained woods are more likely to bow or twist after construction which could cause problems with the tall doors and panels.

The glass and lighting add another $400 to the cost. That adds up to a big chunk of time and money, but this cabinet is built to last and will be proudly passed on to your children's children.

Mill Rough Lumber in Stages

Start by rough sawing your lumber into parts (Photo 1). See the Cutting List (page 119) for the rough cutting dimensions. Most lumber will twist or warp a bit after it's rough cut, so let the rough-sawn parts rest for at least a

Mill the Lumber

This cabinet is solid wood, all the way through.

Rough cut the stiles for the sides, back, doors and legs. Make a couple of extra pieces of each part in case some end up warping badly.

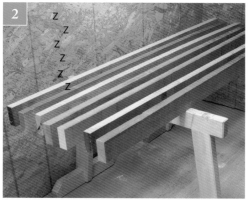

Let your rough-sawn lumber rest for at least 48 hours. Spread out the parts so air can freely circulate around them. Most wood has a tendency to warp or twist a little after it is rough sawn. Letting your rough parts rest allows them to stabilize before you do the final dimensioning.

couple of days before jointing and planing them (Photo 2). It's also a good idea to make a couple extra stiles and legs (A through E) just in case some twist badly. Joint and plane all of the stiles oversize, and let them rest again before final jointing and planing. Then, double-check for flatness before using them (Photo 3). This jointing, planing, resting and checking phase is important and pays off later.

When you're done jointing and planing the parts to thickness and width, you can proceed with cutting the grooves in all the rails and stiles (B through L) (Photo 4). Use a ⅜-in.-by-⅜-in. slot cutter in your router table to make the grooves. You could use a dado blade, but I prefer the slot cutter in a router table because it produces more reliable results.

Next, cut the rails and stiles to final length. Then cut the tongues on the side rails (F and G), the back panel rails

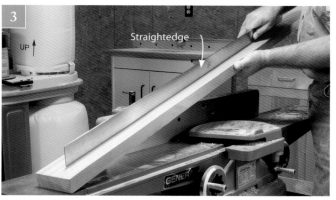

Joint and plane the parts. Let these parts rest for a few days as well. Then use a straightedge to check for flatness. Pick the straightest and flattest boards for the doors.

(H and J) and the back center stile (D). I used a dado blade in the tablesaw for this cut.

Use your miter gauge to push the rails. Cut one side of the tongue, turn it over and cut the other side. Clamp a board to your rip fence as a stop to control the length of the tongue. This scrap board prevents the dado blade from damaging your rip fence.

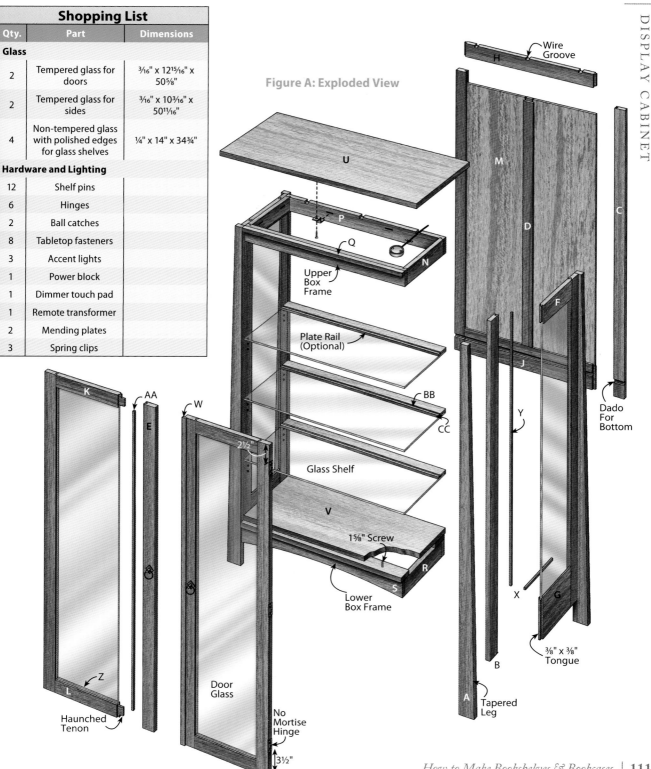

Shopping List

Qty.	Part	Dimensions
Glass		
2	Tempered glass for doors	³⁄₁₆" x 12¹⁵⁄₁₆" x 50⅝"
2	Tempered glass for sides	³⁄₁₆" x 10³⁄₁₆" x 50¹¹⁄₁₆"
4	Non-tempered glass with polished edges for glass shelves	¼" x 14" x 34¾"
Hardware and Lighting		
12	Shelf pins	
6	Hinges	
2	Ball catches	
8	Tabletop fasteners	
3	Accent lights	
1	Power block	
1	Dimmer touch pad	
1	Remote transformer	
2	Mending plates	
3	Spring clips	

Figure A: Exploded View

Wire Groove

H

M

D

C

U

P

Q

N

Upper Box Frame

Plate Rail (Optional)

BB

CC

Glass Shelf

F

J

Y

Dado For Bottom

K

AA

E

W

2½"

V

1⅝" Screw

R

S

Lower Box Frame

X

G

³⁄₈" x ³⁄₈" Tongue

B

A Tapered Leg

Z

L

Haunched Tenon

Door Glass

No Mortise Hinge

3½"

Construction Details

Figure B: Drilling Template for Shelf Pin Holes

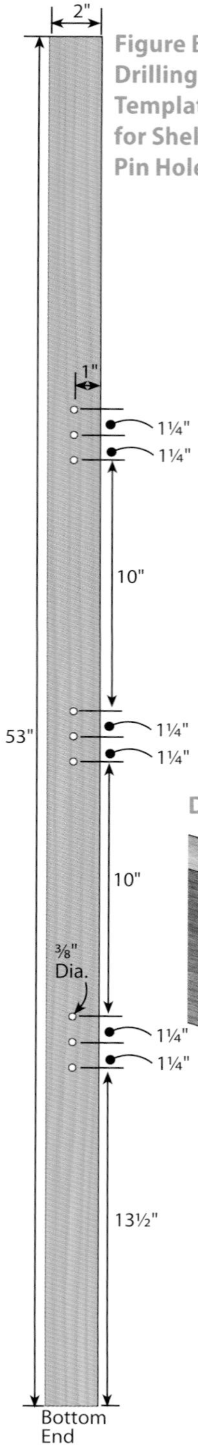
2"
1"
1¼"
1¼"
10"
1¼"
1¼"
53"
10"
⅜" Dia.
1¼"
1¼"
13½"
Bottom End

Detail 1: Cabinet Bottom Showing Lower Box Frame

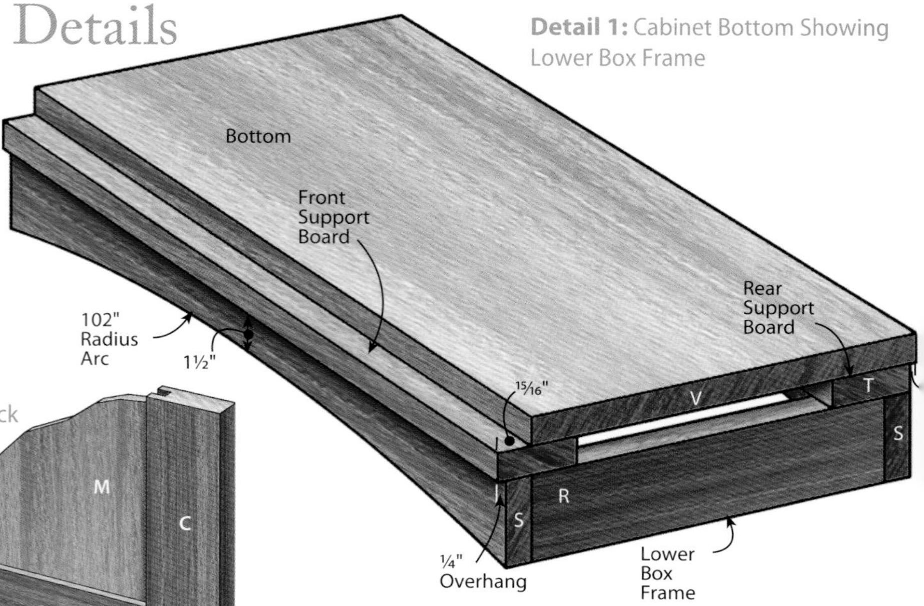
Bottom
Front Support Board
Rear Support Board
102" Radius Arc
1½"
15⁄16"
V
T
S
R
S
¼" Overhang
Lower Box Frame

Detail 2: Cabinet Back

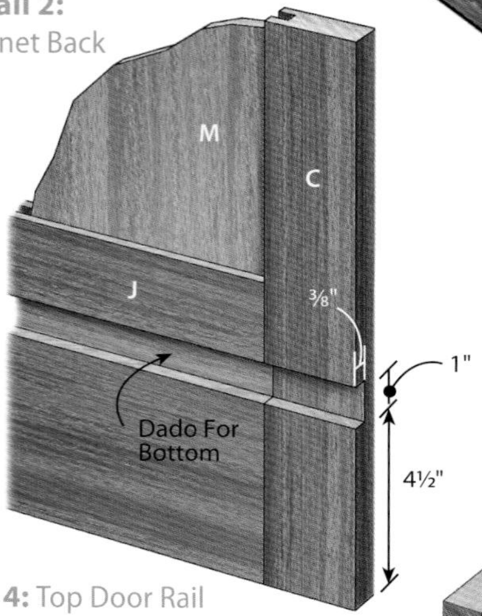
M
C
J
⅜"
1"
Dado For Bottom
4½"

Detail 3: Upper Box Frame

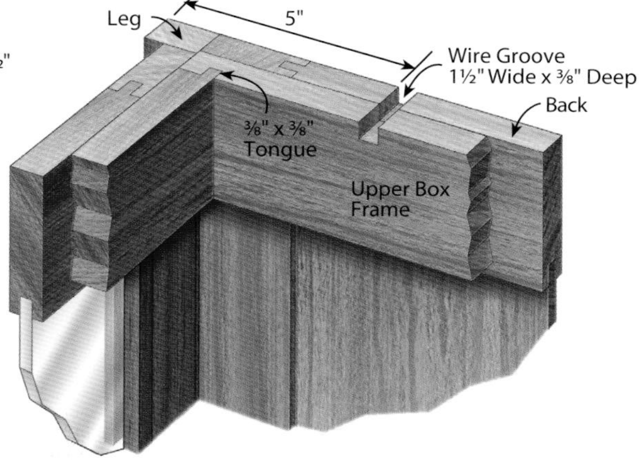
Leg
5"
Wire Groove 1½" Wide x ⅜" Deep
Back
⅜" x ⅜" Tongue
Upper Box Frame

Detail 4: Top Door Rail

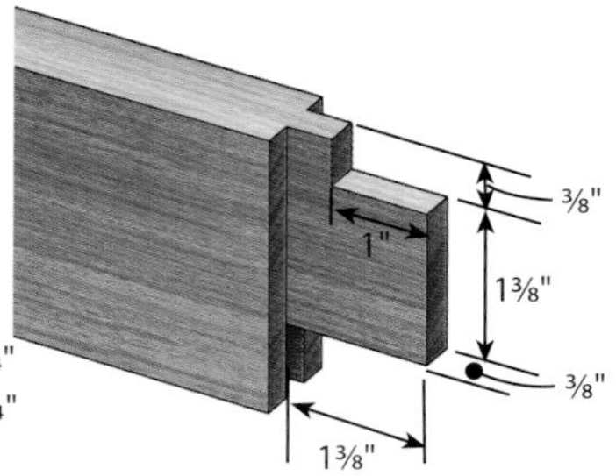
⅜"
1"
1⅜"
⅜"
1⅜"

Detail 5: Bottom Door Rail

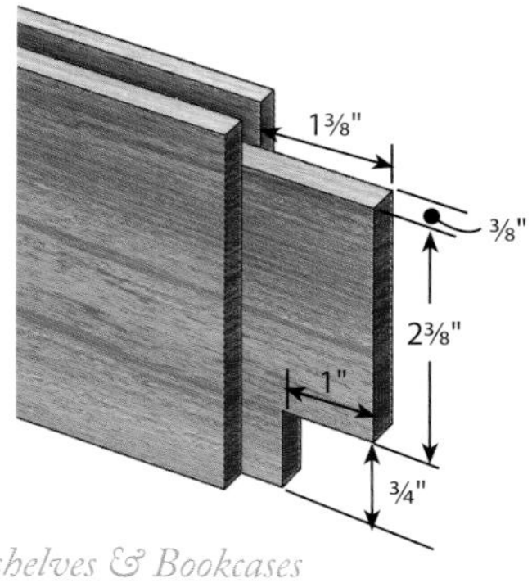
1⅜"
⅜"
2⅜"
1"
¾"

Detail 6: Optional Plate Rail

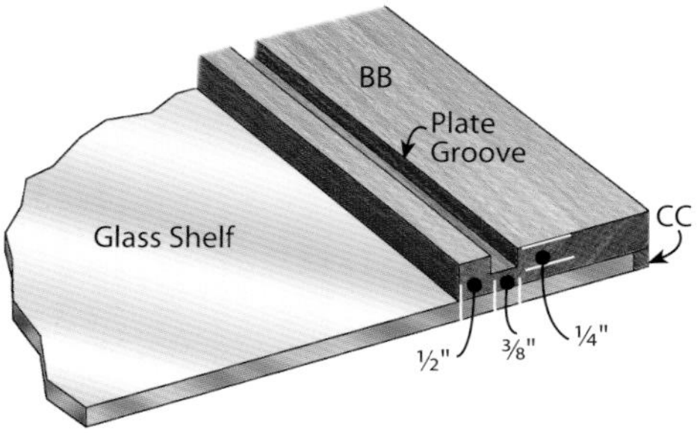
BB
Plate Groove
Glass Shelf
CC
½"
⅜"
¼"

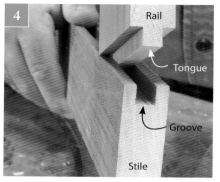

Use a tongue-and-groove joint for the side and back frames. The groove is quick to make on your router table, and the tongue can be cut with a dado head on your tablesaw.

Assemble the side panels on a flat bench. Check for twist by sighting down a pair of winding sticks, which are simply a matching pair of straight boards. Adjust the frame in the clamps until the sticks are parallel.

Glue the tapered legs to the assembled side frames. The legs should be flush with the inside of the side frames. Sand the panel side of the legs and the outside of the side frames before gluing these parts together. If you get any glue squeeze out at these inside corners make sure to clean it up with a damp rag before it dries.

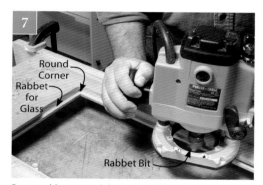

Rout a rabbet around the inside of the side panels for the glass. The router leaves rounded corners, so cut them square with a chisel.

Assemble the Side Frames

Make sure the frames are flat when you glue them up. I assembled the frames on a flat surface and used a pair of winding sticks to check for flatness (Photo 5). If you discover some twist in the frame, loosen the clamp at that corner and raise or lower the corner until the tops of the winding sticks are perfectly parallel. When the glue on the side frames is dry, add the tapered legs (Parts A, Photo 6). Now sand the inside edge of the legs flush with the side frames and rout a ⅜-in.-wide by ⅝-in.-deep rabbet for the glass on the inside of those frames as well (Photo 7).

Make the Box Frames

Start making the box frames by machining the tongue-and-groove joints on parts N, P, R and S (Photo 8). A dado blade works well for making this joint. Next cut the arc on the front rail (U) for the lower box frame and glue and clamp the frames together (Photo 9). When the upper box

Assemble the Case

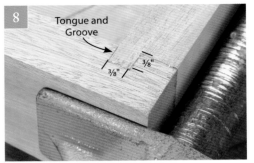

The tongue-and-groove joints at the corners of the box frames provide positive alignment for clamping.

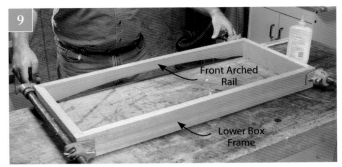

Glue and clamp the box frames. Make sure they are perfectly square and flat, because they determine how square and straight the cabinet ends up.

frame is dry, glue the 1-in. side of the top frame rail (Q) to the front (Fig. A).

Dry clamp the completed box frames to the cabinet sides. Set the lower box frame flush with the bottom of the bottom side rails (Photo 10) and the upper box frame flush with the top of the top side rails (F, Fig. A). The front arched rail (S) should be set back ¼ in. from the front of the legs, but the top frame rail (Q) is set flush with the front of the legs (Photo 10). If your box frames and side panels were accurately made, the cabinet should just about square itself. When everything looks square, take it apart. Sand the inside corner areas between the box frames and cabinet sides and legs, before final gluing. Finally, reclamp and glue sides to box frames (Photo 10).

Assemble the Back

Glue up lumber to make the back panels (M). We simply resawed a couple of 5/4 boards, planed them down and glued them together. The final thickness of the panels is ⅜ in., but leave the material about

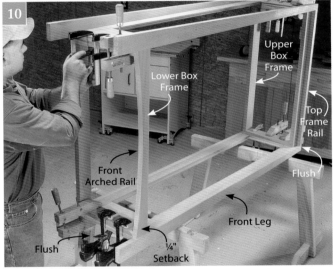

Practice clamping the box frames to the side frames. The box frames add an amazing amount of strength and rigidity to the cabinet. Once you're sure the parts fit square and true, add glue and leave everything clamped until completely dry.

¹⁄₆₄-in. to ¹⁄₃₂-in. thicker. Sand panels before installing them into the back frame.

Glue up the back in stages. Start with the center stile (D) and the top and bottom rails (H and J). Make sure the parts are square to each other. Slide panels (M) into place and add side stiles (C, Photo 11). Check that the back is square and let the glue dry thoroughly.

Assemble the Back

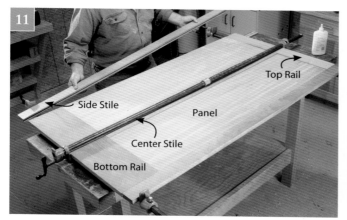

Assemble the frame-and-panel back. First clamp the center stile and top and bottom rails. Then add the panels and the side stiles. Take a dry run at this assembly before actually gluing it.

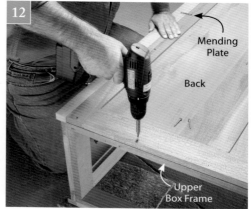

Screw the back to the top and bottom box frames. Add a mending plate along the side to hold the back to the side leg.

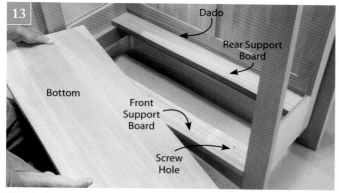

Slide the bottom in place. The bottom is screwed at the front through the front support board and held at the rear by a dado in the back panel. The dado is ⅛-in.-extra deep to allow the bottom to freely shrink and expand.

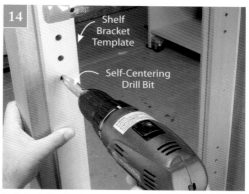

Drill the holes for shelf pins. Using a shop-made template and a self-centering drill bit makes this simple and accurate. Align the template with the inside edge of the side stiles.

Next, rout the groove for the cabinet bottom (V) in the back (Detail 2). Fasten the back to the rest of the cabinet with screws at the top and bottom. Use a 2-in.-long mending plate at each side to keep the back and sides flush (Photo 12).

Add the Bottom and Top

Before installing the bottom (V), glue the support boards (T) to the top of the lower box frame (Detail 1). The bottom is then slid in on top of these support boards. It is held in place with three 1⅝-in. screws through the front support board and in a dado at the back (Photo 13). The bottom extends ¼-in. into the dado. Because the dado is ⅜-in. deep, the solid wood bottom is free to shrink and expand without pushing the back or creating a gap.

Install the Lights

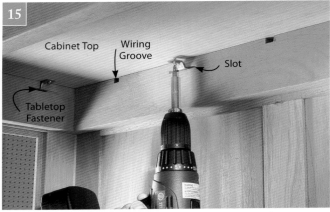

Cabinet Top — **Wiring Groove** — **Slot** — **Tabletop Fastener**

Attach the solid-wood top with tabletop fasteners. This allows the top to expand and contract without cracking. The slots can easily be cut with a plate joiner. Note that wiring grooves have already been routed in the top of the box frame and back.

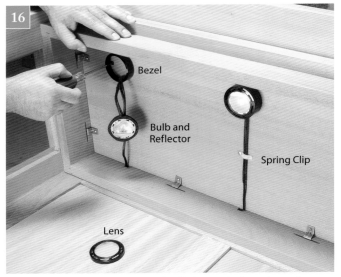

Bezel — **Bulb and Reflector** — **Spring Clip** — **Lens**

Install the low-voltage lights. This style of light is typically made up of a bezel, a bulb and reflector, and the lens. The transformer and switch are then attached to the back of the cabinet.

Test fit all of your parts and hardware before final finishing to prevent surprises.

The top (U) is held in place with tabletop fasteners (Photo 15). They allow seasonal movement of the solid top. Notice that we have pre-routed the grooves for the light-fixture wires.

Install the Lights

Low-voltage halogen accent lights are a good choice for this cabinet. They are easy to install (Photo 16) and relatively inexpensive; $60 for the three lights, transformer, dimmer switch and power block. Simple plastic spring clips hold the wires against the inside of the top.

Always install hardware, including lighting, before final finishing. That way you're sure everything fits correctly.

Drill the holes for the shelf pins (Photo 14) using a drilling template (Fig. B) and a self-centering bit.

Building/Installing Doors

Wood-frame doors with glass need strong joinery to handle the extra weight of the glass. That's why I chose a traditional haunched mortise-and-tenon joint (Photos 17 and 18, and Details 4 and 5). Use winding sticks when gluing and clamping these doors, just like you did with the side panels (Photo 5).

Mount the doors into the cabinet using no-mortise hinges (Fig. A, Photo 19). These hinges greatly simplify door installation. If you've closely followed the sizes in the Cutting List, your doors should fit

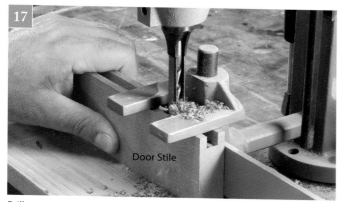

Drill mortises in the door stiles. Center the mortise bit right in the middle of the groove.

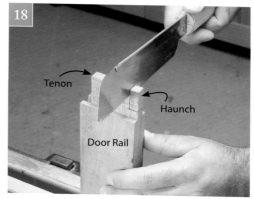

Saw the haunch on the door rail tenons. The haunch will fit into the groove in the door stile and stiffens the mortise-and-tenon joint.

Attach the doors with no-mortise hinges. Put the door in its closed position and mark for the location of the hinges. The doors will likely fit snug at the top and bottom, and that's okay for now. Open the door and install the no-mortise hinges. Because you don't have to fuss with making mortises, their nickname is "the frustration-free hinge."

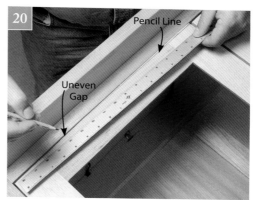

Check the clearance gap along the top and bottom of the doors. Use a ruler as a guide and draw a pencil line for an even gap. Then remove the doors and belt sand to the pencil line.

snug at the top and bottom. The snug fit allows you to trim the tops and bottoms to produce even gaps (Photo 20). The gap at the top and bottom should match the gap on the sides. With the no-mortise hinges, that gap is a little over 1/16 in. Complete the door installation by gluing the astragal strip (W) on the right-hand door. Next add the brass ball door catches and door pulls. Cut the glass retainer strips (X, Y, Z and AA) at this time and if you want to display plates, make the optional plate rails (BB and CC, Detail 6).

Final Assembly

Finishing and Final Assembly

Disassemble your cabinet. Remove the doors, lights, top, bottom and back. Do a final sanding on all the parts and apply the stain and topcoat. We used a red oak stain and wipe-on tung oil finish. When you're done finishing, reassemble the cabinet and install the glass in the doors and sides (Photo 21). Use a brad pusher for this step—it's safer than a hammer.

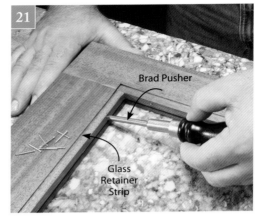

Install the glass and retainer strips after you have stained and finished all of the cabinet parts. Predrill small holes in the retainer strip and then use a brad pusher to install the small brads. The brad pusher is a lot safer than a hammer around glass.

Taking the Twist Out of Tall Doors

When building frame-style doors, it's always important to mill your lumber carefully and assemble the doors so they turn out as flat as possible. But inevitably, some doors twist and don't hang flat after installation. This is especially true of tall doors. Anticipating this, we added a couple of details to our doors to overcome any potential twist. The astragal strip and the strong catches work together to hold both doors securely closed and flat.

Use a strong catch on the right-hand door. This brass ball catch can even hold a moderately twisted door flat and keeps the doors securely closed.

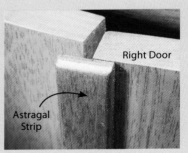

Use an astragal strip to hold the left-hand door shut. It also covers up the center gap between the doors.

Cutting List

Overall Dimensions: 66½" H x 43" W x 19½" D

Part	Name	Qty.	Rough Dimensions T x W x L	Final Dimensions T x W x L	Notes
Legs and Stiles					
A	Legs	4	5⁄4" x 3½" x 67"	1" x 3" x 65½"	Tapered one side from 3" at bottom to 1½" at top
B	Side stiles	4	5⁄4" x 3½" x 67"	⅞" x 2½" x 61"	
C	Back side stiles	2	5⁄4" x 3½" x 67"	⅞" x 2½" x 61"	
D	Back center stile	1	5⁄4" x 3½" x 67"	⅞" x 2½" x 50¾"	Groove both edges, length includes tongues at both ends
E	Door stiles	4	5⁄4" x 3½" x 67"	⅞" x 2½" x 55¹⁵⁄₁₆"	
Rails					
F	Side rails- top	2	5⁄4" x 4" x 12"	⅞" x 3½" x 10¼"	Length includes tongues
G	Side rails- bot.	2	5⁄4" x 8" x 12"	⅞" x 7½" x 10¼"	Length includes tongues
H	Back rail- top	1	5⁄4" x 4" x 32"	⅞" x 3½" x 30¾"	Length includes tongues
J	Back rail- bot.	1	5⁄4" x 8" x 32"	⅞" x 7½" x 30¾"	Length includes tongues
K	Door rails - top	2	5⁄4" x 3" x 17"	⅞" x 2½" x 15⅛"	Length includes tenons
L	Door rails - bot.	2	5⁄4" x 4" x 17"	⅞" x 3½" x 15⅛"	Length includes tenons
Back Panels					
M	Back panels	2	⅝" x 16" x 52"	⅜" x 14⅜" x 50⅝"	Glued up from narrower boards
Box Frames					
N	Upper- sides	2	5⁄4" x 3½" x 16"	1" x 3" x 13⁷⁄₁₆"	Length includes tongues
P	Upper- front, back	2	5⁄4" x 3½" x 36"	1" x 3" x 35"	
Q	Front top rail	1	5⁄4" x 1½" x 36"	1" x ¹⁵⁄₁₆" x 35"	
R	Lower - sides	2	5⁄4" x 3½" x 16"	1" x 3" x 14⅛"	Length includes tongues
S	Lower - frt., bk.	2	5⁄4" x 3½" x 36"	1" x 3" x 35"	Front part is arched
T	Support boards	2	5⁄4" x 4" x 36"	1" x 3" x 35"	
Top and Bottom					
U	Top	1	5⁄4" x 21" x 45"	1" x 19½" x 43"	Glued up from narrower boards
V	Bottom	1	5⁄4" x 16" x 36"	1" x 14¹⁵⁄₁₆" x 35"	Glued up from narrower boards
Astragal Strip and Glass Retainer Strips					
W	Astragal strip	1		¼" x ⅞" x 56"	Trim length to fit final door height
X	Glass retainer	4		⅜" x ⅜" x 9½"	Side panel rails
Y	Glass retainer	4		⅜" x ⅜" x 50¾"	Side panel stiles
Z	Glass retainer	4		⅜" x ⅜" x 12¼"	Door rails
AA	Glass retainer	4		⅜" x ⅜" x 50¹¹⁄₁₆"	Door stiles
Plate Rails (Optional)					
BB	Board	3		½" x 3" x 34¾"	
CC	Shelf hook	3		¼" x ¼" x 34¾"	

No need to lug a big cabinet from your shop to the living room. This bookcase breaks down into easy-to-handle components.

Building the Center Cabinet

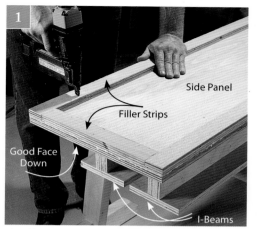

Glue filler strips to one side panel. Add a few brad nails to keep the filler strips from sliding. Locate brad nails near the inside edge of the fillers so they don't interfere when the panels are cut to final size later. The second side panel goes on top of this assembly.

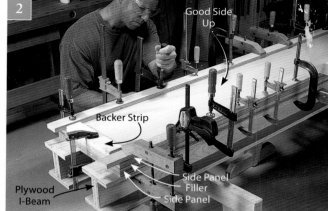

Beg, borrow or buy two dozen clamps. Add some backer strips to protect the good side of your plywood. Then, clamp the whole sandwich to the plywood I-beams.

Materials for our bookcase, including hardware, cost about $1,500. If you substitute plain-sliced red oak for the rift-sliced white oak, your total cost will be about $700.

Building the Center Cabinet

Start by roughing out the plywood parts. Pay special attention to the Notes section of the Cutting List (page 137). This section tells you how much to add to the length and width measurements for the necessary waste. The amount you add, which gets sawn or routed off later, varies from part to part.

Making the Built-up Panels

To assemble your first sandwich, lay a side panel (C1), with its good side down, on the plywood I-beams (Photo 1). Add some glue, and brad nail the filler strips (C2, C3) in place. The brad nails just have to keep

the fillers from slipping when clamped, so you don't need very many. And don't worry if the filler strips don't line up perfectly with the edges of the side panel. The whole sandwich gets cut to final size later on. Apply glue to the top side of these fillers and add the next panel (C1), good side up this time. Add some backer strips to protect the wood and clamp the three-layer plywood sandwich to the lip of the I-beams (Photo 2).

Cutting the Sandwiched Parts to Final Size

Before you cut the sandwiched parts to final size, it's a good idea to remove excess glue drips from the edges of the sandwiches. A paint scraper works great. If you don't remove them, these hardened drips will hang up on your saw's fence, causing an uneven cut.

Building the Center Cabinet

Figure B: Plywood I-Beams

These I-beams provide a strong, flat surface for clamping. It takes only one sheet of plywood to make them. We glued, clamped and stapled our I-beams together but screws will do the job, too. Just make sure all fasteners are well sunk or they will scratch your project.

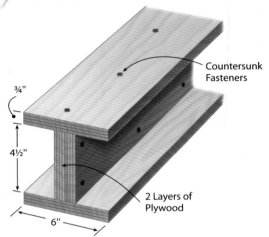

¾"

4½"

6"

Countersunk Fasteners

2 Layers of Plywood

Plywood I-beams ensure that the panels are glued up perfectly flat.

Figure C: Flat-Panel Door

We used a tongue-and-groove router bit set to make the door parts.

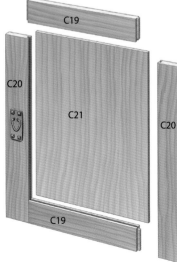

C19

C20

C20

C21

C19

Detail 1: Valance

The valance is glued to the cabinet top. This assembly is then screwed to the side panels.

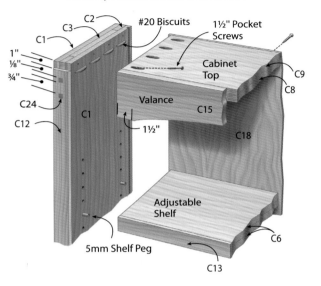

C2

C3

C1

#20 Biscuits

1½" Pocket Screws

Cabinet Top

C9

C8

1"
⅛"
¾"

C24

Valance

C15

C18

C1

C12

1½"

Adjustable Shelf

C6

5mm Shelf Peg

C13

Detail 2: Toe Board

The toe board is glued to the cabinet bottom. The bottom's edge banding aligns with the back of the chamfer.

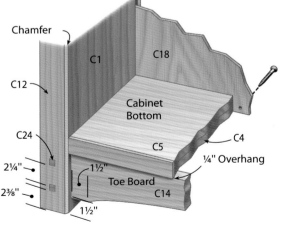

Chamfer

C1

C18

C12

Cabinet Bottom

C24

C5

C4

¼" Overhang

2¼"

2⅜"

1½"

Toe Board

C14

1½"

Building the Center Cabinet

Figure D:
Center Cabinet

Combining biscuits and pocket screws makes the knockdown joinery simple and strong.

Detail 3:
Cabinet Cross Section
The cabinet back is installed in side dadoes but overlaps the cabinet top and bottom.

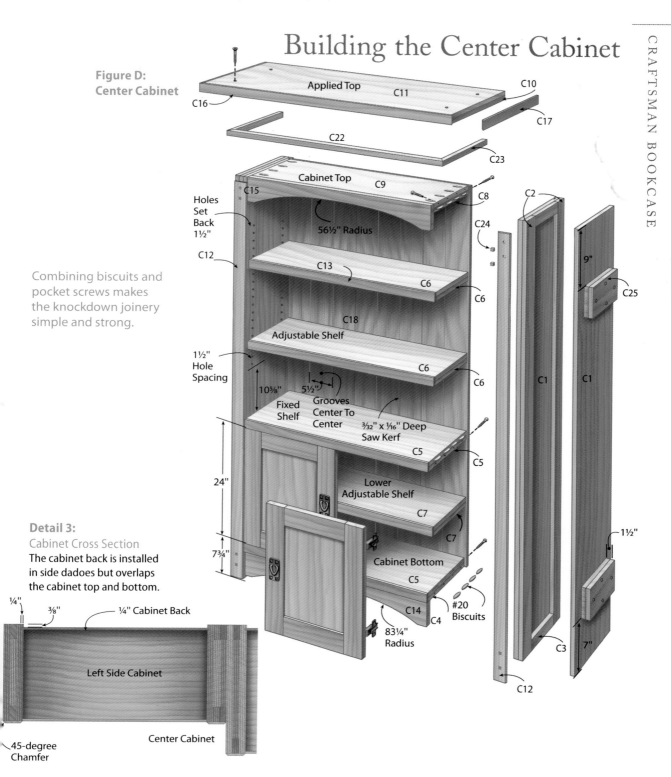

Applied Top   C11
C16
C10
C17
C22
C23
Cabinet Top   C9
C15
C8
Holes Set Back 1½"
56½" Radius
C24
C2
C12
C13
C6
9"
C6
C6
C25
Adjustable Shelf   C18
1½" Hole Spacing
C6
C6
C1
C1
10⅝"
5½"
Fixed Shelf
Grooves Center To Center
³⁄₃₂" x ¹⁄₁₆" Deep Saw Kerf
C5
C5
Lower Adjustable Shelf
24"
C7
C7
1½"
Cabinet Bottom
C5
7¾"
C14
83¼" Radius
C4
#20 Biscuits
C3
7"
C12

¼"
⅜"
¼" Cabinet Back
Left Side Cabinet
45-degree Chamfer
Center Cabinet

Building the Center Cabinet

Now rip the parts to final width on your tablesaw. Try to saw an equal amount from each side of the sandwich.

Trimming the panels to length is done with a router (Photos 3 and 4). Trim some off both ends, just as you did with the sides. When making trim cuts, use multiple passes to give you a smoother cut that is easier on your router.

Making the Shelves

The shelves are made up of two layers of plywood. Use the I-beams to make sure these parts end up flat. Cut shelves to width and trim to length.

Making Edge Banding

To conserve material when making the ¼-in.-thick edge banding, resaw a ¾-in. board in half and plane the two parts to thickness. Use this edge banding on all the sandwiched panels (Photo 5). When you're done edge banding, put a bottom-bearing trim bit in your router and trim the edge banding flush. Use a fine-tooth handsaw to trim the overhang at the ends.

Now use a handsaw and a chisel to cut a notch in the top end of the edge banding (C12) (Photo 6). A piece of trim (C22) fits in this notch later on. Next, add a block to the bottom of each side panel. Get out your router again and install a 45-degree chamfering bit. Rout the bevels into the edge banding (C12) of the side panels (see Oops! page 127).

Trimming sides to length is a two-step process.

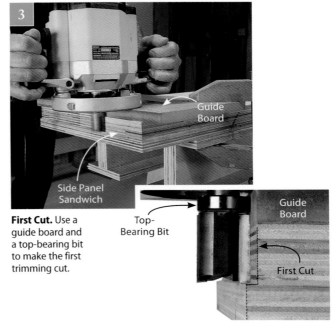

First Cut. Use a guide board and a top-bearing bit to make the first trimming cut.

Second Cut. Flip the panel over and trim the remaining edge with a bottom-bearing bit. The bottom-bearing bit will run on the previously routed surface.

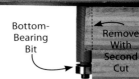

Building the Center Cabinet

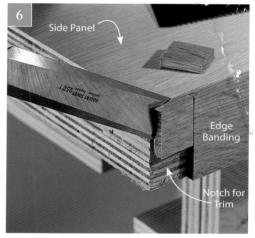

Glue and clamp edge banding to each panel. The edge banding overhangs the ends and sides a little, and will be trimmed later. Make sure to use a backer board to protect the edge banding from the clamps.

Saw and chisel a notch at the top end of the edge banding on the side panels. A piece of trim will fit in this notch later.

Oops!

While routing the bevels on the sides of our prototype bookcase we oopsed. Because the router had less support at the corner, it tipped and gouged the edge banding. While reacting to this tipping we routed around the corner. Unfortunately, this is one oops that can't be sanded out (see photo at right).

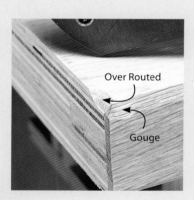

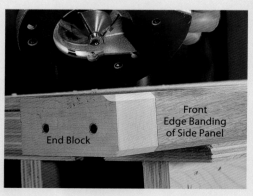

Screwing a block to the end of the panels solves both problems: it provides more support for the router and eliminates the possibility of routing around the corner (see photo at left).

Building the Center Cabinet

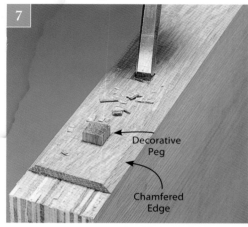

Chisel ¼-in.-deep mortises for the decorative pegs. Glue and hammer the pegs into place. Trim the pegs flush using a fine-tooth handsaw.

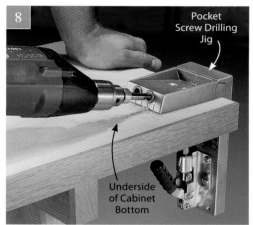

Drill pocket screw holes in the cabinet's bottom, top and fixed shelf. Pay special attention to which side you drill the screw pockets into. A mistake here is difficult to fix.

Adding the Pegs and Making Dadoes

Add the decorative pegs by chiseling mortises (Photo 7) and gluing and hammering the pegs in place. Once the glue has set, trim the pegs flush with a fine-tooth handsaw. Later, when you finish sand, you can remove any saw marks.

Now it's time to cut the dadoes in the side panels for the ¼-in. back (Detail 3). Clearly mark your two upright panels left and right and then mark where the dadoes go. Cut the dadoes with a dado head on your tablesaw or a router with an edge guide.

Drilling and Cutting the Knockdown Joinery

The knockdown joinery we've built into this project is a combination of pocket screws and dry-fit biscuits. The biscuits provide alignment between the parts and the pocket screws pull everything together good and tight.

First, take some time to examine all the cabinet parts and clearly mark the locations for the pocket-screw holes. Double-check your marks because a mistake here will be difficult to fix. Drill the pocket screw holes using a pocket-screw jig (Photo 8). Now, cut the biscuit slots (Photo 9).

Making the Arched Toe and Valance Boards

You need to make a paper pattern to trace the arched shape on the toe and valance boards (Photo 10). Use your bandsaw or jigsaw to cut the arches. Smooth the saw marks with a file or drum sander.

Glue the toe board to the cabinet bottom (Photo 11) and the valance to the cabinet top (Detail 1).

Building the Center Cabinet

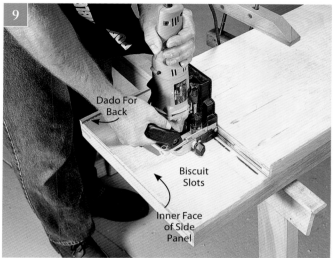

Cut the biscuit slots in the side panel and the cabinet bottom. By lining up the bottom and side and clamping them together, they act as a guide for the biscuit cutter.

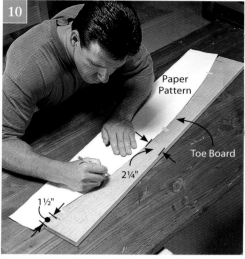

Trace arcs onto the toe and valance boards. The arcs stop 1½ in. from each end.

Assembling the Main Cabinet

Now that you have all the sandwich parts fabricated, you can dry assemble the cabinet (Photo 12). Install the biscuits, *without glue*, and pocket screw the parts together. When all the parts are screwed together, place padding on the floor and lay the cabinet down on its face.

It's time to make the back (C18). The kerfs in the back are made on the tablesaw using a thin-kerf (³⁄₃₂ in.) saw blade. A standard ⅛-in.-kerf blade will work too, if you prefer wider lines. After you've made the kerfs, slide the back into the dadoes along the cabinet sides. Check the cabinet for square by measuring corner to corner (Photo 13). Attach the back by screwing it to the top and the bottom and to the fixed shelf.

Adding the Applied Top

With the back panel in place, stand the cabinet up and screw the applied top in place, centered and flush with the back edge of the sides. Make sure to install it with the birch side up and the oak side down. Trace around the top edge of the cabinet with a pencil (Photo 14). This line is used to position the trim strips that are glued to the applied top (Photo 15).

Drilling for Shelf Pins

Make a shelf-pin drilling guide from a piece of ½-in.-thick wood. Drill ⁷⁄₁₆-in.-diameter guide holes in this board at the appropriate locations (see Fig. D). Clamp this guide to the cabinet side to prevent it from slipping. Use a 5mm self-centering bit to drill the shelf pin holes (Photo 16).

Building the Center Cabinet

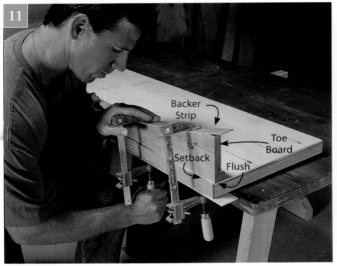

11

Backer Strip

¼" Setback

Toe Board

Flush

Glue and clamp the toe board to the cabinet bottom. Set the toe board back the thickness of the edge banding. Use backer strips to protect your work.

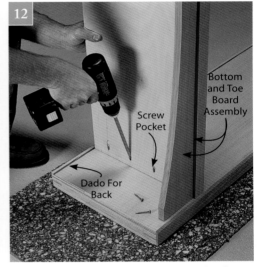

12

Bottom and Toe Board Assembly

Screw Pocket

Dado For Back

It's time to assemble. Just add the biscuits and pocket screws. Do not glue.

Adding the Doors

There's nothing tricky about these doors. We used a tongue-and-groove router bit set, but they could be doweled together or assembled with mortises and tenons.

The doors are hung on Euro-style hinges (Photo 17). These hinges have the big advantage of being easy to adjust up and down, left and right, and in and out. Installing Euro-style hinges does, however, require the use of a 35mm drill bit.

Side Cabinets

The side cabinets are built like the center cabinet except for a couple of important differences: The inner side panels (S1) are open on one side (Fig. G) and the outer side panels (S2) are tapered.

There are three important construction details to understand before building these unique tapered panels. The first is that they need to be cut and built to final width. They're 3½-in. thick, which is too thick to saw on most 10-in. tablesaws. The second detail is that the panel sandwiches are made with tapered fillers. Making these tapered fillers requires a special tapering sled for your planer. Finally, trimming the tapered sandwiches to final length requires a shimmed guide board to accommodate the tapers.

Building the Center Cabinet

Check the cabinet for square by measuring from corner to corner. The diagonal measurements should be the same. If you need to, bump the cabinet a little to make it square, then screw the back in place.

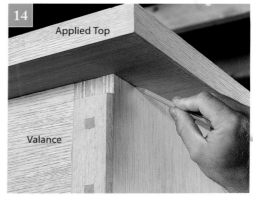

Trace around the cabinet to mark the location for the trim strips that get glued to the applied top.

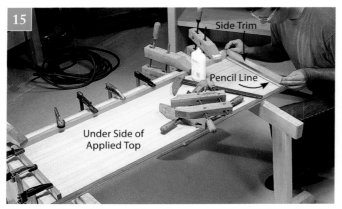

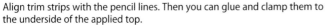

Align trim strips with the pencil lines. Then you can glue and clamp them to the underside of the applied top.

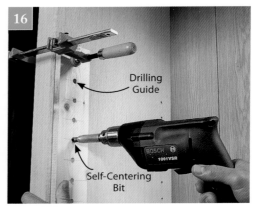

Drill shelf peg holes using a shop-made drilling guide and a self-centering bit.

Hang the doors with Euro-style hinges. They make door installation and adjustment a real snap.

Building the Side Cabinets

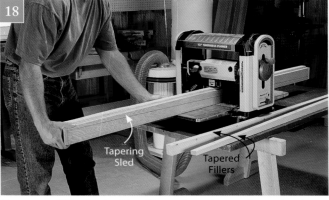

Plane tapered fillers for the side cabinets using a shop-made tapering sled.

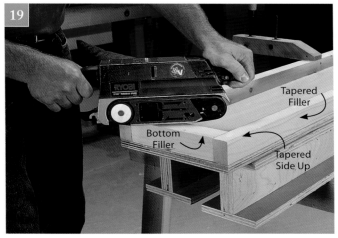

Sand horizontal fillers to match the slight angle of the tapered fillers. Add the outside panel, then glue and clamp.

Without question, making the tapered sides is the most difficult part of this project. We've tried to simplify the process a bit with these step-by-step directions. First, build the tapering sled for your planer (Fig. E). The 1½-in.-thick material for the fillers is made from two pieces of ¾-in. stock, glued together. When the glue is dry, joint one edge and rough cut the taper on the bandsaw. Use the tapering sled to plane the fillers to final size (Photo 18). Mark the tapered sides of the fillers.

Now you can glue up the tapered sandwiches. Start by gluing and clamping the tapered fillers (tapered side up) to one of the plywood sides. This makes it easier to keep the edges aligned, which is important because these side panels are already cut to final width. Next, add the short horizontal fillers. When the glue is dry, sand these short fillers to match the angle of the vertical fillers (Photo 19). Complete the sandwich by adding the other plywood side. Make sure to mark this top panel as the

Figure E: Tapering Sled

Make this sled out of ¾-in. birch plywood.

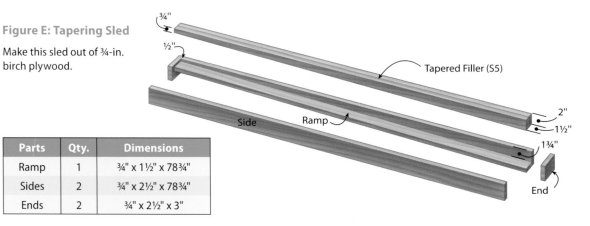

Parts	Qty.	Dimensions
Ramp	1	¾" x 1½" x 78¾"
Sides	2	¾" x 2½" x 78¾"
Ends	2	¾" x 2½" x 3"

Building the Side Cabinets

tapered side. Now repeat this process for the other tapered side.

The next step is to trim the top and bottom of these panels to final length. Lay the panel, tapered side up, and clamp the shimmed guide board to the bottom (thick) end of the panel (Photo 20). Make the trim cut with a top-bearing bit. Next go to the top end of the panel and use the shimmed guide board again. The angle here is on the opposite side, so place the shim under the router side of the guide board this time. Now flip the panel over and use the bottom-bearing bit to complete the trimming. No shimming is needed because this is the straight (inside) face of the panel.

Making the Drawers

We made our drawer boxes out of ⅝-in.-solid lumber and joined the sides with biscuits (Fig. H). Our drawer slides required a ½-in. installation clearance on each side, so we sized the drawer parts accordingly. With the drawer boxes installed, drill the holes for the screws that will hold the drawer fronts in place. Use nickels and double-face tape to align and attach the drawer fronts until the screws are added (Photo 21).

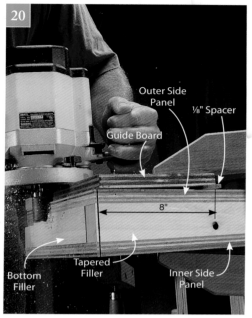

Trimming the tapered sides requires a shimmed guide board for the first cut. Use this board on the tapered face of the panels only. Trim the inside face with a bottom-bearing bit, as shown in Photo 4.

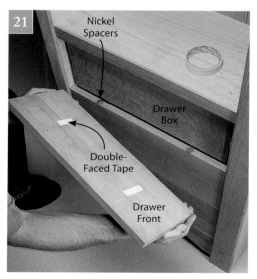

Position the drawer fronts and temporarily hold them in place with double-faced tape. A couple of nickels used as spacers provide just the right amount of clearance between the drawer fronts.

Building the Side Cabinets

Figure F: Plywood Cutting Diagrams

For our bookcase we used:
- 7 sheets of ¾-in. rift-sliced plywood
- 1 sheet of ¼-in. rift-sliced plywood (C21, S28)
- 2 sheets of ¼-in. plain-sliced plywood (S24, C18)
- 3 sheets of ¾-in. birch plywood
- We also used about 55 bd. ft. of rift-sawn white oak.

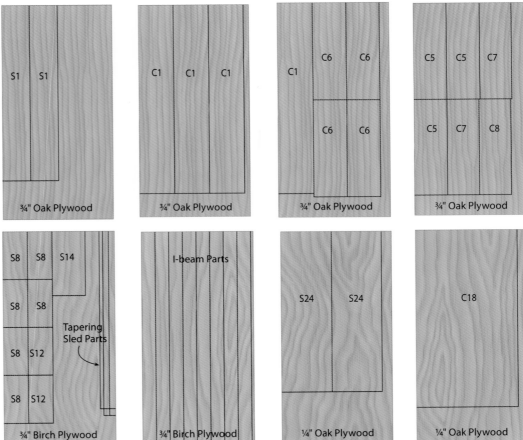

Building the Side Cabinets

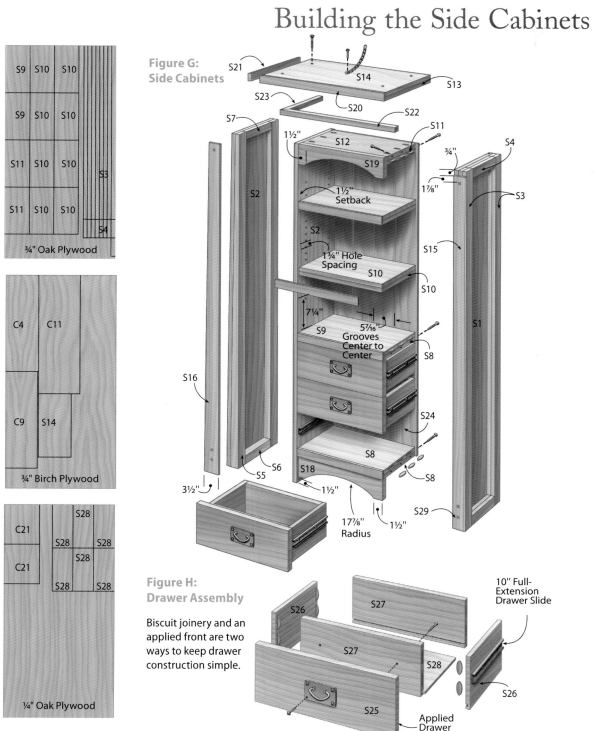

Figure G:
Side Cabinets

¾" Oak Plywood

S9	S10	S10
S9	S10	S10
S11	S10	S10
S11	S10	S10

S3
S4

¾" Birch Plywood

| C4 | C11 |
| C9 | S14 |

¼" Oak Plywood

C21	S28
	S28	S28
C21	S28
	S28	S28

S21
S14
S13
S23
S20
S7
S22
S11
S4
1½"
S12
S19
¾"
1⅞"
S3
S2
1½"
Setback
S15
S2
1¾" Hole
Spacing
S10
S10
7¼"
5⁷⁄₁₆"
Grooves
Center to
Center
S9
S8
S1
S16
S24
S8
S6
S18
S8
S5
3½"
1½"
S29
17⅞"
Radius
1½"

Figure H:
Drawer Assembly

Biscuit joinery and an
applied front are two
ways to keep drawer
construction simple.

S26
S27
10" Full-
Extension
Drawer Slide
S27
S28
S26
S25
Applied
Drawer
Front

Finishing and Installation

Staining and finishing is a breeze because the knock-down design allows each part to be finished separately.

Attaching the cabinets is as simple as a two-piece jigsaw puzzle. Line up the side cabinet with the alignment blocks and slide them together. The cabinets are then secured with a couple of screws from inside the side cabinet.

Finishing

One of the best things about this cabinet's knockdown joinery is you can finish all the parts separately.

We used two coats of Minwax Early American oil stain and top coated it with a couple coats of Minwax tung oil. Tung oil is an easy-to-use wipe-on finish that can be built up to a rich luster. The more you add the more shine you get.

Final Setup

Another benefit of this knockdown design is that you don't have to lug the completed cabinet from your shop to its final destination. With a helper, you can have this cabinet installed in less than two hours.

Start with the center cabinet. Assemble it, stand it up, and set it in its final location. Then do the side cabinets. These interlock with the center cabinet via the alignment blocks (Photo 23). From inside

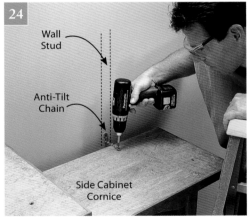

Attach the anti-tilt chain between the top of each side cabinet and a wall stud. For cabinets this tall, this is essential for safety.

the side cabinets, a couple of screws into the alignment blocks will hold the units together. Now get a stepladder and add the anti-tilt chains (Photo 24). Because this bookcase is tall and shallow these must not be overlooked. Finally, add the shelves, doors, drawers and hardware.

Cutting List

Overall Dimensions: 86¾" H x 105½" W x 18½" D

Part	Qty.	Name	Material	Dimensions T x W x L	Notes
Center Cabinet					
C1	4	Side panels	Oak plywood	¾" x 15¼" x 85¼"	Add 1" to length and ½" width for rough cutting.
C2	4	Vertical fillers	Oak plywood	¾" x 1¾" x 85¼"	Add ½" to length for rough cutting.
C3	4	Horizontal fillers	Oak plywood	¾" x 1¾" x 12¼"	
C4	1	Underside of cabinet bottom	Birch plywood	¾" x 14⅜" x 43½"	Add ½" to length and width for rough cutting.
C5	3	Upper side of cabinet bottom / both parts of fixed shelf	Oak plywood	¾" x 14⅜" x 43½"	Add ½" to length and width for rough cutting.
C6	4	Upper adjustable shelf parts	Oak plywood	¾" x 14⅜" x 43⁷⁄₁₆"	Add ½" to length and width for rough cutting.
C7	2	Lower adjustable shelf parts	Oak plywood	¾" x 13⅝" x 43⁷⁄₁₆"	Add ½" to length and width for rough cutting.
C8	1	Underside of cabinet top	Oak plywood	¾" x 13⅞" x 43½"	Add ½" to length and width for rough cutting.
C9	1	Upper side of cabinet top	Birch plywood	¾" x 13⅞" x 43½"	Add ½" to length and width for rough cutting.
C10	1	Under side of applied top	Oak plywood	¾" x 18¼" x 53½"	Add ½" to length and width for rough cutting.
C11	1	Upper side of applied top	Birch plywood	¾" x 18¼" x 53½"	Add ½" to length and width for rough cutting.
C12	2	Edge banding for sides	Oak	¼" x 2¼" x 85¼"	Add ½" to length and ¼" to width for rough cutting.
C13	5	Edge banding for cabinet bottom and shelves	Oak	¼" x 1½" x 43½"	Add ½" to length and width for rough cutting.
C14	1	Toe board	Oak	¾" x 4¾" x 43½"	
C15	1	Valance board	Oak	¾" x 7" x 43½"	
C16	1	Front edge banding for applied top	Oak	¼" x 1½" x 54"	Add ½" to length and ¼" to width for rough cutting.
C17	2	Side edge banding for applied top	Oak	¼" x 1½" x 18½"	Add ½" to length and ¼" to width for rough cutting.
C18	1	Back	Oak plywood	¼" x 44" x 79"	
C19	4	Door rails	Oak	¾" x 3⁹⁄₁₆" x 15⅜"	Dimensions make doors that fit the opening exactly. Joint doors for clearance after assembly.
C20	4	Door stiles	Oak	¾" x 3⁹⁄₁₆" x 24"	
C21	2	Door panels	Oak plywood	¼" x 15⅜" x 17⅝"	
C22	1	Front trim strip	Oak	¾" x 1" x 49½"	

Cutting List (continued)
Overall Dimensions: 86¾" H x 105½" W x 18½" D

Part	Qty.	Name	Material	Dimensions T x W x L	Notes
Center Cabinet *continued*					
C23	2	Side trim strips	Oak	¾" x 1" x 16"	
C24	8	Pegs	Oak	½" x ½" x ¼"	Add ¼" to length for rough cutting.
C25	4	Alignment blocks	Oak plywood	1½" x 5" x 8⅜"	Glued up from two layers of ¾" plywood.
Side Cabinets					
S1	2	Panels for inner sides	Oak plywood	¾" x 11½" x 78¼"	Add ½" to length and ⅜" to width for rough cutting.
S2	4	Panels for tapered sides	Oak plywood	¾" x 11½" x 78¼"	Add ½" to length for rough cutting, cut to exact width.
S3	8	Vertical fillers for inner sides	Oak plywood	¾" x 1¾" x 78¼"	Add ½" to length for rough cutting.
S4	8	Horizontal fillers for inner sides	Oak plywood	¾" x 1¾" x 8⅜"	
S5	4	Vertical fillers for tapered sides	Pine or poplar	2" x 1½" x 78¼"	Glued up from two layers of ¾" wood.
S6	2	Bottom horizontal fillers for tapered sides	Pine or poplar	2" x 1½" x 8½"	Glued up from two layers of ¾" wood.
S7	2	Top horizontal fillers for tapered sides	Pine or poplar	¾" x 1½" x 8½"	
S8	6	Both sides of cabinet bottom/ underside of fixed shelf	Birch plywood	¾" x 10⅝" x 21¼"	Add ½" to length and width for rough cutting.
S9	2	Upper sides of fixed shelf	Oak plywood	¾" x 10⅝" x 21¼"	Add ½" to length and width for rough cutting.
S10	8	Adjustable shelf parts	Oak plywood	¾" x 10⅝" x 21³⁄₁₆"	Add ½" to length and width for rough cutting.
S11	2	Under sides of cabinet top	Oak plywood	¾" x 10⅝" x 21¼"	Add ½" to length and width for rough cutting.
S12	2	Upper sides of cabinet top	Birch plywood	¾" x 10⅝" x 21¼"	Add ½" to length and width for rough cutting.
S13	2	Under sides of applied top	Oak plywood	¾" x 14½" x 28½"	Add ½" to length and width for rough cutting.
S14	2	Upper sides of applied top	Birch plywood	¾" x 14½" x 28½"	Add ½" to length and width for rough cutting.
S15	2	Edge banding for inner sides	Oak	¼" x 2¼" x 78¼"	Add ½" to length and width for rough cutting.
S16	2	Edge banding for tapered outer sides	Oak	¼" x 3½" x 78¼"	Add ½" to length and width for rough cutting.
S17	8	Edge banding for cabinet bottom and shelves	Oak	¼" x 1½" x 21¼"	Add ½" to length and width for rough cutting.
S18	2	Toe boards	Oak	¾" x 4¾" x 21¼"	

Part	Qty.	Name	Material	Dimensions T x W x L	Notes
Side Cabinets *continued*					
S19	2	Valance boards	Oak	¾" x 5" x 21¼"	
S20	2	Front edge banding for applied top	Oak	¼" x 1½" x 28¾"	Add ½" to length and ¼" to width for rough cutting.
S21	2	Side edge banding for applied top	Oak	¼" x 1½" x 14¾"	Add ½" to length and ¼" to width for rough cutting.
S22	2	Front trim strips	Oak	¾" x ¾" x 26½"	
S23	2	Side trim strips	Oak	¾" x ¾" x 12¼"	
S24	2	Backs	Oak plywood	¼" x 21¾" x 72"	
S25	6	Drawer fronts	Oak	¾" x 7⅞" x 21¹⁄₁₆"	Allows for ³⁄₃₂" clearance around drawer fronts.
S26	12	Drawer box sides	Oak	⅝" x 7" x 10"	Based on using biscuit joinery.
S27	12	Drawer box fronts and backs	Oak	⅝" x 7" x 19"	
S28	6	Drawer bottoms	Oak plywood	¼" x 9¼" x 19½"	Based on ¼" deep dadoes in drawer sides.
S29	12	Pegs	Oak	½" x ½" x ¼"	Add ¼" to length for rough cutting.

by DAVID RADTKE

Floor-to-Ceiling Bookcase

CREATE A CLASSIC LOOK WITH READY-MADE MOLDINGS

I f you're bursting at the seams with books and collectibles to display, here's a bookcase that maximizes space, fits any room, and uses lumberyard moldings.

A Flexible Design

We designed this bookshelf without a back or base unit to make it easier to fit into any room. You can build around vents and outlets by simply shifting a standard (the upright piece supporting a shelf). This only affects the length of the shelves, which is not difficult to change in the Cutting List (page 143).

Without a base or back, will the bookshelf be sturdy? Sure, because hidden steel pins made from lag bolts go right into the floor and hold the standards rigid (Photo 8).

Are your floors and walls out of square? Not a problem. We've engineered this project to work even if your room is a bit out of kilter. The moldings are applied individually to each standard and cover any gaps resulting from uneven floors or walls.

Use Shortest Height for Measurement

Measure the height and width of your wall. Note the locations of all receptacles, switches and vents. If they're in the way, modify our design by relocating a standard and changing the length of the shelves.

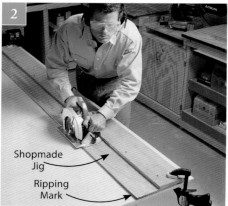

Shopmade Jig

Ripping Mark

Rip the plywood into strips for the standards. Although you can use a tablesaw to make these cuts, you won't have to struggle with a bulky sheet of plywood if you use a circular saw and a simple cutting jig.

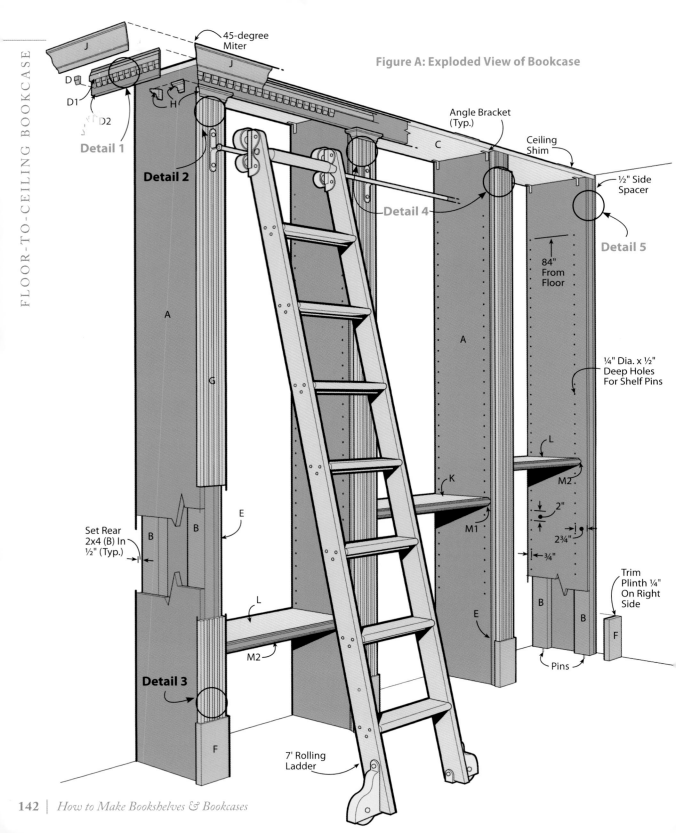

Figure A: Exploded View of Bookcase

45-degree Miter

J

J

D

D1

D2

Detail 1

H

Detail 2

Angle Bracket (Typ.)

C

Ceiling Shim

½" Side Spacer

Detail 5

Detail 4

84" From Floor

A

A

G

¼" Dia. x ½" Deep Holes For Shelf Pins

K

L

M2

2"

M1

2¾"

Set Rear 2x4 (B) In ½" (Typ.)

B

B

B

E

¾"

Trim Plinth ¼" On Right Side

B

B

F

L

M2

E

Detail 3

F

Pins

7' Rolling Ladder

Cross Sections

Detail 1

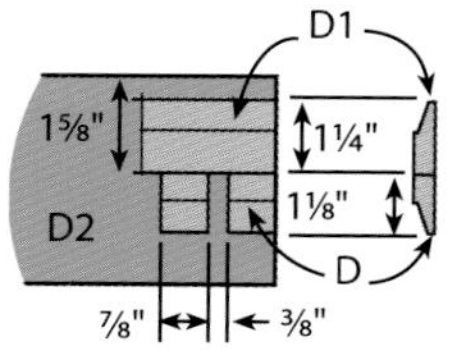
D1
1⅝"
1¼"
1⅛"
D2
D
⅞"
⅜"

Detail 2

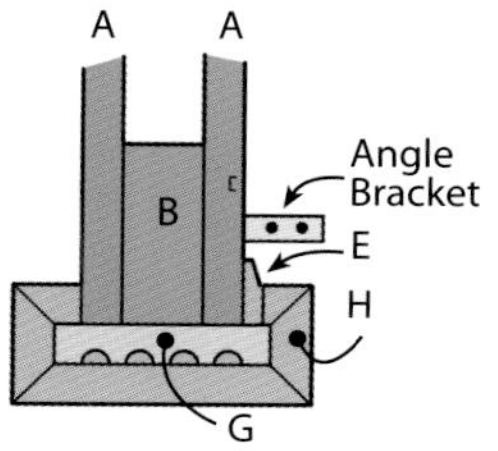
A
A
B
Angle Bracket
E
H
G

Detail 3

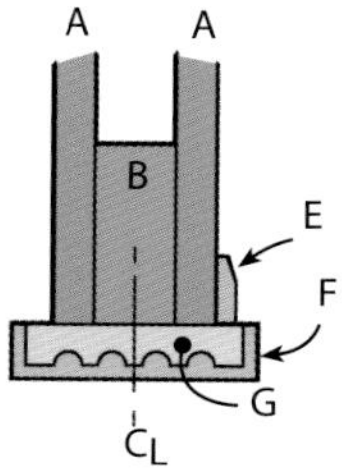
A
A
B
E
F
G
CL

Detail 4

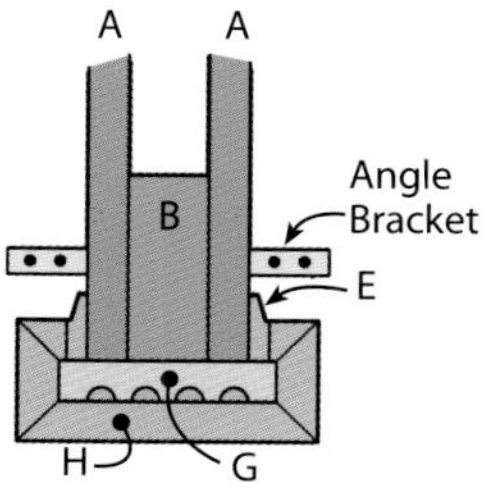
A
A
B
Angle Bracket
E
H
G

Detail 5

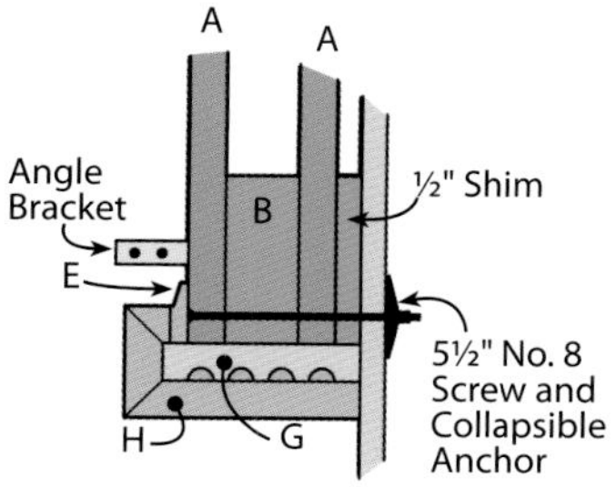
A
A
Angle Bracket
B
½" Shim
E
5½" No. 8 Screw and Collapsible Anchor
H
G

Detail 6

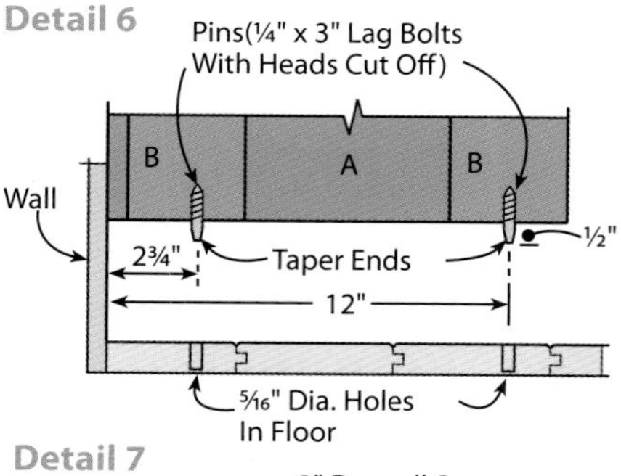
Pins(¼" x 3" Lag Bolts With Heads Cut Off)
B
A
B
Wall
½"
2¾"
Taper Ends
12"
5⁄16" Dia. Holes In Floor

Detail 7

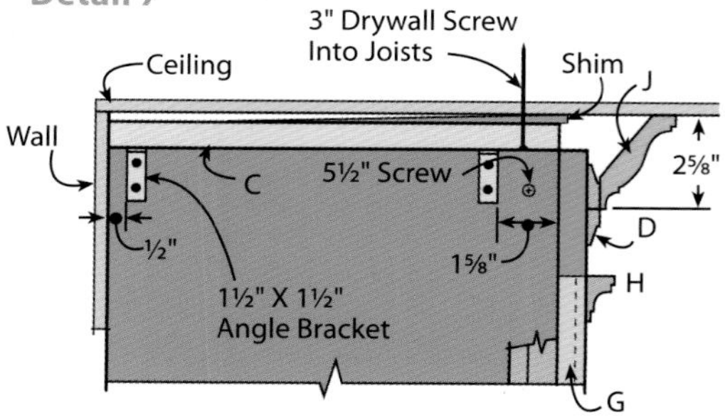
3" Drywall Screw Into Joists
Ceiling
Shim
J
Wall
C
5½" Screw
2⅝"
D
½"
1⅝"
1½" X 1½" Angle Bracket
H
G

Figure B: Casings and Moldings

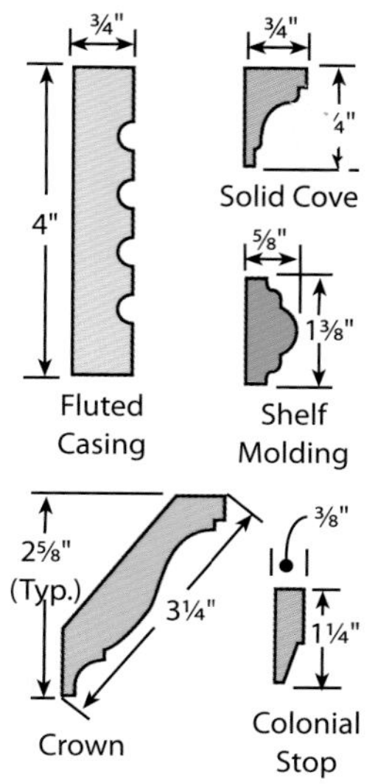
¾"
4"
Fluted Casing
¾"
¼"
Solid Cove
⅝"
1⅜"
Shelf Molding
2⅝" (Typ.)
3¼"
Crown
⅜"
1¼"
Colonial Stop

Cutting List

Overall Dimensions: 8' H x 8' L x 14¾" D

Part	Qty.	Name	Material	Dimensions	Comments
A	8	Face	Plywood	¾" x 13¾" x 96"	Trim length is 1-in. less than the distance from floor to ceiling.
B	8	Brace	2x4	2" x 4" x 96"	Same as above.
C	1	Top	Plywood	¾" x 13¾" x 96"	Trim length to fit.
D	a.n.	Dentils	Colonial stop	⅜" x 1¼" x ⅞"	Rip 10-ft. long, 1¼-in. wide molding to 1⅛-in. Then cut dentils to length.
D1	2	Filler strip	Colonial stop	⅜" x 1¼"	Cut 10-ft.-long piece to fit.
D2	2	Backer boards		¾" x 3½"	Cut 10-ft.-long piece to fit.
E	6	Molding	Colonial stop	⅜" x 1¼"	Cut 8-ft.-long pieces to fit.
F	4	Plinth blocks		1 1⁄16" x 4½" x 8"	
G	4	Casing	Fluted casing	¾" x 4"	Cut 7-ft. pieces to fit.
H	a.n.	Cove	Cove molding	¾" x 1¼"	Cut from 8-ft. length.
J	2	Crown	Crown molding	2⅝" tall	Cut from 10-ft. length.
K	7	Middle shelves	Plywood	¾" x 11⅜" x 32"	Trim length is 3⁄16-in. less than distance between standards.
L	14	Outer shelves	Plywood	¾" x 11⅜" x 26"	Same as above.
M1	7	Shelf molding	Shelf molding	⅝" x 1⅜" x 32"	Same as above.
M2	14	Shelf molding	Shelf molding	⅝" x 1⅜" x 26"	Same as above.

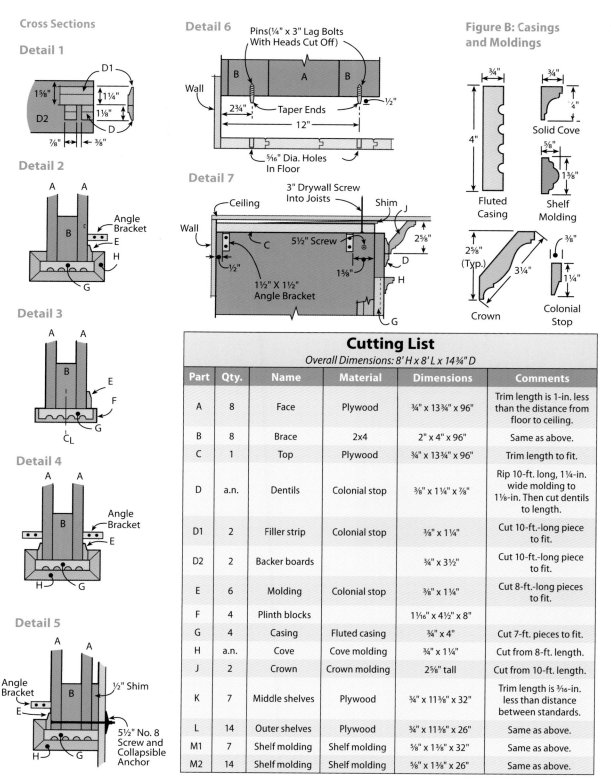

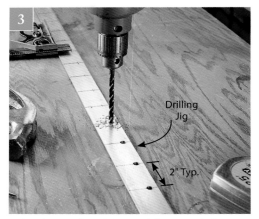

Make a foolproof, durable jig to drill accurate holes for the shelf-support pins. Drill ¼-in.-dia. holes into a 1¼ in. x ⅛ in. x 6-ft. piece of aluminum or steel bar stock (available at hardware stores).

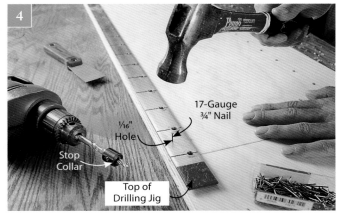

Nail the jig to the plywood through four small holes drilled along the jig's length. Identify the top of the jig with paint or tape, then align the top hole with a line 84 in. from the plywood's bottom (see Fig. A). Drill ¼-in. holes ½-in. deep through each of the jig holes using a stop collar to limit the hole's depth. Remember, the end standards don't require holes.

Glue 2x4s between the plywood pieces to create the standards. Be sure the front 2x4 is flush with the front edge of the panels and the rear 2x4 is set in about ½ in. After assembling, scribe the standard to fit the wall, if necessary. The ½-in. overhang on the back makes scribing much easier.

Easy Molding

A large built-in requires a lot of molding, so we've chosen a mixture of classic shapes that you can buy through a lumberyard or home center. We special-ordered the maple moldings for our bookcase, but if you build yours from oak or pine, molding to match is readily available. We'll show you how to modify one molding to make an impressive cornice, complete with dentils (Photo 10).

This bookcase blends right into your room reusing your existing baseboard molding. Simply cut your molding and reinstall it between the standards.

Figure C: Locations of Floor Pins (Top View)

Receptacles and floor vents are the bane of most built-ins, but not this one. Just locate the standards so they miss the obstacles.

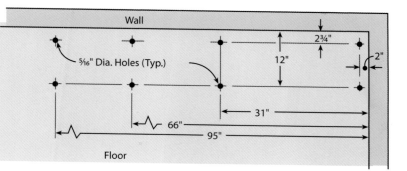

Wall

⁵⁄₁₆" Dia. Holes (Typ.)

2¾"

12"

2"

31"

66"

95"

Floor

Planning Your Bookcase

This built-in bookcase is easy to enlarge, work-around windows, or change in any way to suit your room. Before you buy your lumber, carefully measure your selected site. Take into consideration the height, width and any obstructions unique to your room.

The center section of our bookcase is 6 in. wider than the two outer sections. This establishes a focal point, and the two side sections provide symmetry. Keep in mind that you can move the standards closer together or add a standard or two to fit a longer wall.

If you move the standards to accommodate outlets or air vents, note that the standards should never be farther than 36 in. apart. This is the maximum distance for sag-free shelves and safe installation of the rolling-ladder hardware.

Use a level to check for irregularities like a sloping floor or an uneven wall. If they're not too far off, the standards won't need altering. But if your walls and floor are way out of whack, you'll be able to scribe the

standards on the backside and bottom, and then cut along your scribe for a perfect fit.

Our bookcase was built onto a wood floor. If you have carpeting, you'll need to pull back the carpet and pad and reinstall them later around the base of the bookcase. And yes, the ladder will roll on carpeting.

6

Cut Lag Screw

3" Lag Screw

Leg

Install a pair of pins to hold the bottom of the standard into holes you'll drill in the floor (Fig. A, Detail 6). Make the pins from 3-in. lag screws. Use a wrench to turn them until the threads are all inside the bottoms of the 2x4s. Then cut off the heads of the screws with a hacksaw and file a slight taper on the bottom of the protruding pin.

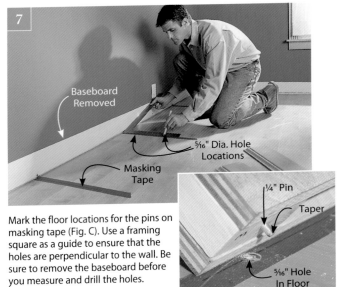

7

Baseboard Removed

⁵⁄₁₆" Dia. Hole Locations

Masking Tape

¼" Pin

Taper

⁵⁄₁₆" Hole In Floor

Mark the floor locations for the pins on masking tape (Fig. C). Use a framing square as a guide to ensure that the holes are perpendicular to the wall. Be sure to remove the baseboard before you measure and drill the holes.

8

Top Measurement

Temporary Brace

Bottom Measurement

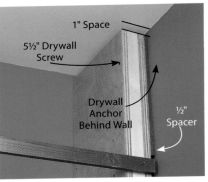

1" Space

5½" Drywall Screw

Drywall Anchor Behind Wall

½" Spacer

Tip the standards into position. Each standard should be plumb and equally spaced, top and bottom.

Start with the standard that goes in the corner, facing the wall (see inset). If the wall isn't plumb, nail shims onto the spacers fastened to the standard's side to compensate. Fasten the standard to the wall with long drywall screws and anchors (Fig. A, Detail 5).

Next, tip the second standard into the holes in the floor. Have an assistant hold the standard in place while you make sure it's plumb and the top and bottom measurements are equal. When everything's lined up, lock the standard in place with a temporary brace.

9

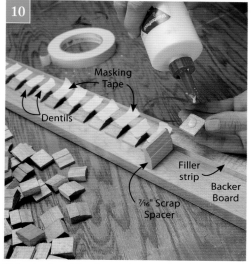

10

Masking Tape

Dentils

Filler strip

Backer Board

7/16" Scrap Spacer

Note: You may have to use a stud finder to locate the ceiling joists, or install blocks between joists in the attic.

Slide the cabinet top over the standards and secure it in place with angle brackets (Fig. A). Shim the gaps between the top and the ceiling. Screw the top to the ceiling joists in three locations using two screws at each location.

Make dentil molding from Colonial-style stop molding (Fig. B). You could start from scratch, but this is much easier. First, glue and nail a long piece of molding (the filler strip) to a backer board. Then cut individual dentils from a long strip of molding and glue them onto the backer board with a small dab of glue (Fig. A, Detail 1). Use a scrap piece of molding as a spacer.

Tip

Selecting Lumber

Look for straight 2x4s for the standards. If you can't find any, cut up the best ones you can find into 2-ft. lengths and sandwich these shorter pieces between the plywood pieces. You don't need a continuous 2x4 for strength.

Oops!

My dentil molding needs some dental work! I glued one of the dentils in crooked, and it spoiled the whole look of the molding.

To remove the offending piece, I warmed it up slightly with a heat gun to loosen the glue. (Both white and yellow glues soften up and let go when they're warmed.) Then I pried off the dentil with a thin putty knife. Presto! I'm back in business with a new tooth.

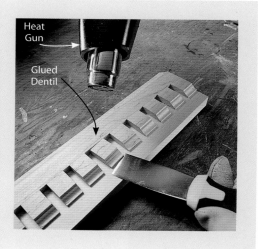

Heat Gun

Glued Dentil

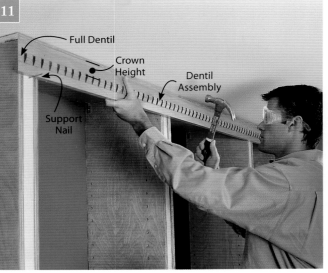

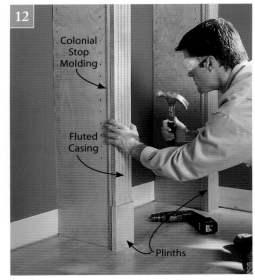

Miter the end of the dentil assembly. Leave a full dentil at the miter, then cut the assembly to length. Nail it to the front of the standards with 6d finish nails. Maintain a consistent distance from the top of the dentils to the ceiling. This space must match the height of your crown molding (Fig. A, Detail 7).

Prefinish all of the parts in your shop to keep the mess and smells under control.

Nail molding to the front of the standards with 6d finish nails (Fig. A, Detail 3). Nail the plinth blocks at the bottom first. (Because the plinth blocks are wider than the fluted casing, you'll need to rip ¼ in. from the width of the block that's against the wall.) Nail the Colonial stop molding even with the fronts of the standards; then apply the fluted casing.

Shopping List

Item	Qty
¾" x 4' x 8' plywood	5
2x4 x 8' pine	8
1x2 x 10' pine, for braces	1
1x4 x 10' board, same as molding	1
⅜" x 1¼" x 10' colonial stop	2
⅜" x 1¼" x 8' colonial stop	6
1¹⁄₁₆" x 4½" x 8" plinth blocks	4
¾" x 4" x 7' fluted casing	4
⅝" x 1⅜" x 8' shelf molding	7
1¼" x 8' cove molding	1
3¼" x 10' crown molding	1
¼" peg-style shelf brackets	84

Item	Qty
1¼" x ⅛" x 6' bar stock	1
1½" x 1½" angle brackets w/screws	12
Yellow glue	1 qt.
¾" 17-gauge nails	1 pkg.
1¼" x 17-gauge brads	1 pkg.
4d, 6d and 8d finish nails	1 lb. ea.
Minwax wood conditioner	2 qts.
Minwax No. 245 pecan stain	2 qts.
Minwax satin polyurethane	2 qts.
Colored putty stick	1
¼" x 3" lag bolts	8
Collapsible anchors	4

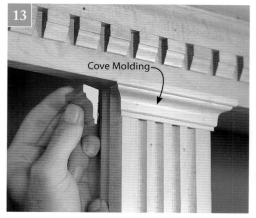

13

Glue mitered cove molding to the tops of the fluted casing. The cove molding should wrap around to meet the Colonial stop molding (Fig. A, Details 2, 4 and 5).

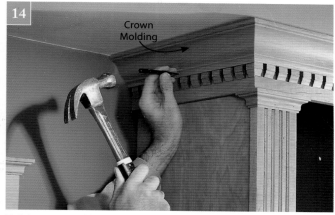

14

Nail the crown molding onto the dentil assembly. Miter each end at the outside corner and butt the other ends against the wall. Use 4d finish nails every 12 in. and drive them below the surface of the wood with a nail set.

15

Optional: Install the rolling ladder hardware to the face of the cabinet according to the manufacturer's instructions.

We spent about $600 on materials for the bookcase shown here. The optional ladder and hardware cost an additional $700 to $1,200, depending on how fancy it is. Before you make sawdust, check out our advice on Planning Your Bookcase (page 145). Then follow Photos 1 through 15 for the nitty gritty how-to.

Finishing

Finish the standards, molding and shelves before installation. This keeps spills and obnoxious fumes out of your living space. After the bookcase is completely installed, you can touch up any cut ends with stain and fill nail holes with colored putty.

For a blotch-free, even color on this birch, we applied Minwax Wood Conditioner before staining. Then we used Minwax No. 245 pecan stain to blend the maple and birch pieces. Finally, we applied a polyurethane varnish for durability.

Size and Cost

We designed this bookcase to fit into a typical room with an 8-ft. ceiling and at least 8 ft. of wall space, something like a typical bedroom you may want to convert to a library or home office. You can enlarge this bookcase simply by adding standards.

by D A V I D   R A D T K E

Craftsman-Style Bookcases and Mantel

ENHANCE YOUR HOME WITH THIS BUILT-IN CLASSIC

The Craftsman architectural movement of the early 20th century is enjoying a resurgence in popularity both in furniture design and home accessories. These bookcases and fireplace surround reflect that tradition.

If you can build a basic box with a face frame, then you can build this project. The tapered columns that showcase the hearth and buttress the bookcases present the greatest challenge. We'll show you a couple nifty jigs that make even that process seem easy.

When it comes to installing the bookcases, we solved the age-old problem of fitting a cabinet into an alcove by adding a 3-in. filler strip to the outside stile of each bookcase. Filler strips are a great way to bridge the gap between the cabinet and the wall. They're easy to install and they look great. You put the strips on at the very end, sawing, planing and sanding to a perfect fit. The result? The bookcase and mantel look as if the house were built around them!

We used quarter and rift-sawn oak—both solid and veneer plywood—for this project. This wood is a hallmark of the Craftsman style.

This project was designed for fireplaces that have a drywall or plaster enclosure, similar to the one shown here. The mantel portion of the design doesn't lend itself well to a brick fireplace.

The wood dividers (or muntins) at the top of the bookcase door frames are not "true" muntins. They don't frame individual panes of glass, but rather slip over a single pane. It's less authentic, but a lot easier.

This is a big project and is best approached in phases. The mantel and fireplace surround comprise the first phase. The two bookcases can be handled later.

You'll need a tablesaw, bandsaw, planer, biscuit joiner (a pocket-screw or doweling jig will also work) and a router with a flush-trim bit. A compressor and a finish nailer make installation a whole lot easier. In the end, expect to spend around $2,000 for the entire project.

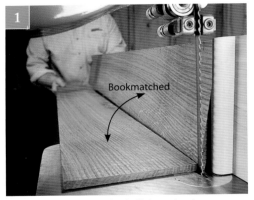

Resaw a 6-in.-wide board in half, then glue the two halves together to create a bookmatched panel for the front of the columns.

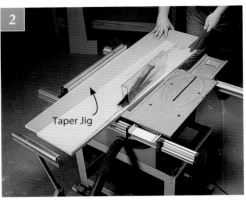

Glue the bookmatched oak panel to the tapered plywood. Then cut the excess on the bandsaw leaving a 1/16-in. overhang on the sides. Trim the facing flush to the sides with a router and a flush-trim bit.

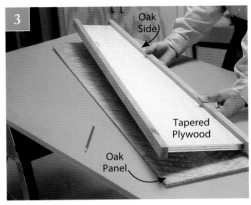

Cut the tapered plywood on a tablesaw using two simple tapering jigs (Fig. A). Glue solid oak sides to the column.

Getting Started

Start by measuring the fireplace projection and the area on each side of the fireplace. Our design is configured for the specific space shown in Fig. C. To allow room for the columns, we widened the mantel to extend beyond the original fireplace projection. You'll no doubt have to alter our plan to suit your own room. Here are a couple of things to keep in mind:

- You can widen the bookcases without making the doors too big by adding a center divider between the doors.
- If you don't have walls at the cabinet ends, attach oak plywood end panels similar to the wall returns (parts L). Extend the cabinet tops (parts U1) and apply additional banding to cover the edge of the return.
- If you need to alter the mantel to fit a different projection, be sure to maintain adequate setbacks from the fireplace opening (see Safety Considerations (page 155)).
- Have the tiles you're going to use on hand before you build. 8 in. x 8-in. tiles can vary by 1/4-in. and you'll need accurate measurements for making the mantel face frame.

Building the Tapered Columns

1. Resaw oak for the bookmatched panel (N2) (Photo 1).

2. Cut the tapered plywood (M) using the jigs in Fig. A and Photo 2.

3. Glue the oak sides (N1) to the edges of the tapered plywood (Fig. D, Detail 1).

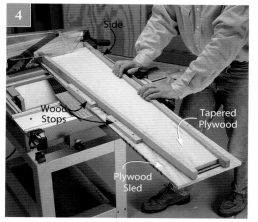

Trim the oak sides flush with the bottom of the tapered plywood. Make a ¾ in. x 12 in. x 48 in. plywood sled with wood stops to center the column. Add a long fence to your miter gauge and use it to guide the sled through the saw.

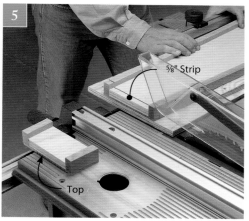

Cut the column top, then remove an additional ⅝-in. section to make room for the astragal (see Photo 6). The ⅝-in. strip, plus the ⅛-in. saw kerf, create a ¾-in. gap that gets filled by the astragal.

4. Assemble the columns (Photo 3).

5. Trim the ends of the oak sides flush with the top and bottom of the tapered plywood (Photo 4 and 5).

6. Cut a 3-in. section from the top of the column. Then, remove a ⅝-in.-wide strip to make room for the ¾-in. astragal (P) (Photo 5).

7. Cut the column astragals (P).

8. Assemble the column backers with parts C and D.

9. Assemble the mitered column base fronts and sides (parts Q and R) with glue and nails.

10. Attach the column base, bottom, astragal and top to the column backer (Photo 6).

Figure A: Tapering Jigs

Build two jigs to cut the tapered plywood. Cut the notches in each jig with a bandsaw or jigsaw. Use Jig A. to make the first cut. Then flip the plywood over and cut the second taper using Jig B.

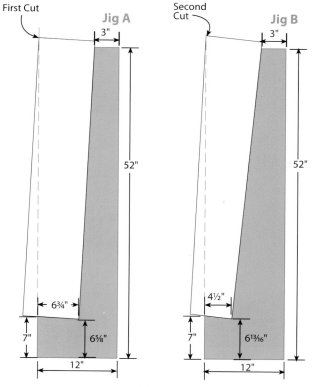

Figure C: Bookcase and Mantel Assembly

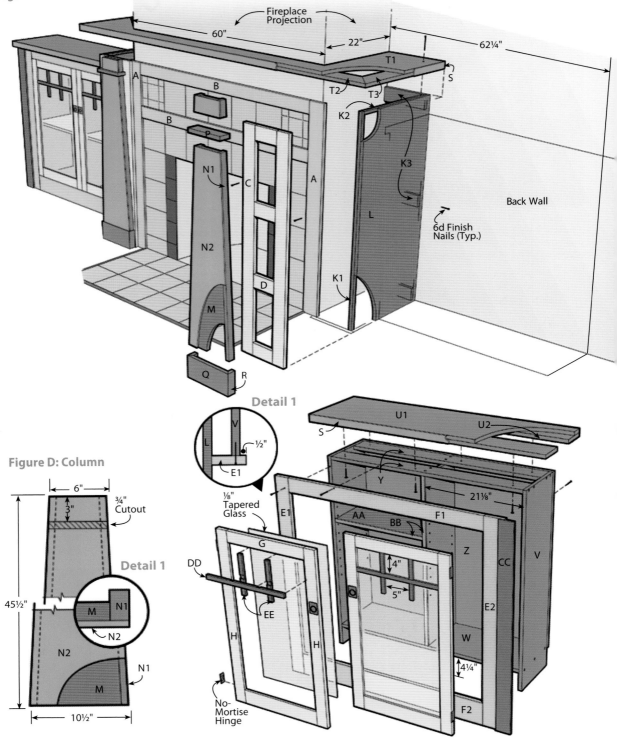

Fireplace Projection

60"

22"

62¼"

T1

T2

T3

S

K2

K3

A

B

B

P

N1

C

N2

A

D

K1

L

M

6d Finish Nails (Typ.)

Back Wall

Q

R

Detail 1

V

L

½"

E1

Figure D: Column

6"

¾" Cutout

3"

45½"

Detail 1

M

N1

N2

N2

N1

M

10½"

⅛" Tapered Glass

E1

U1

U2

S

Y

21⅛"

AA

BB

F1

G

Z

4"

5"

CC

V

DD

E2

EE

W

H

H

4¼"

F2

No-Mortise Hinge

Safety Considerations

For safety and convenience, don't overlook these items when planning and installing your project:

- Fire codes generally require that ¾-in.-thick wood be kept 6 in. away from the edge of a fireplace opening to prevent radiant heat from scorching it. For wood protruding 1½ in. or more, such as the front columns of this project, the wood must be at least 12 in. away.
- Set the new tile or stone around the fireplace front and hearth.
- Put electrical receptacle box extenders on any electrical boxes that end up behind the cabinet. Don't remove the covers and bury the receptacles in the wall. It violates electrical codes. The extender slips over the receptacle, extends inside the box and covers the cut-out in the plywood backs of the cabinets, as shown here. Be sure to shut off the power to the box you're working on.
- Hire a licensed electrician to install new electrical receptacles in the cabinet bases or in the floor to make up for the receptacles left inside the cabinets.
- The glass in the bookcase doors must be either safety glass (plastic film between two thin layers of glass) or tempered glass. This reduces the danger of injury from broken glass.

Figure B: Outlet Extender

Outlet extenders allow you to safely extend wall outlets through the cabinet back.

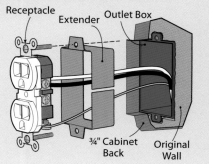

Receptacle
Extender
Outlet Box
¾" Cabinet Back
Original Wall

Figure E: Mantel Installation

Screw the columns to the face frame and the wall returns to the columns. Slide the whole assembly against the wall and nail the wall returns to the wall cleats and the face frame to the fireplace projection.

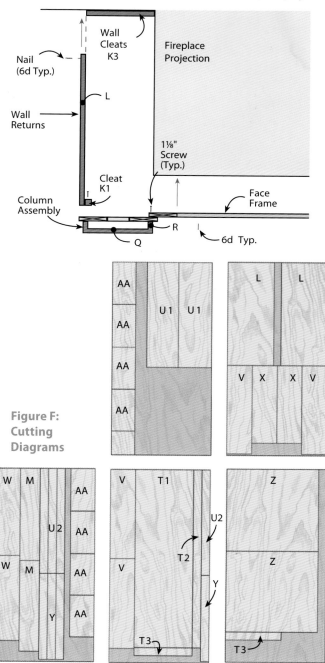

Wall Cleats K3
Fireplace Projection
Nail (6d Typ.)
L
Wall Returns
1⅛" Screw (Typ.)
Cleat K1
Column Assembly
Face Frame
R
Q
6d Typ.

Figure F: Cutting Diagrams

AA
AA
AA
AA
U 1 U 1
L L
V X X V

W M
AA
U 2
AA
W M
AA
Y
AA

V T 1
U2
T 2
V
Y
T 3

Z
Z
T 3

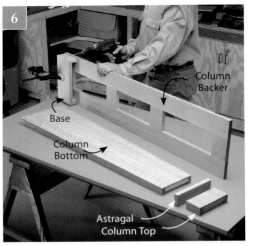

Screw the column parts on the column backer starting with the base and working up. Drill pilot holes and screw them in place from behind.

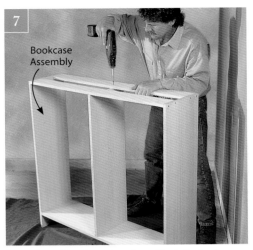

Screw the cabinet boxes together. Attach the backs using screws every 6 in. The cabinet backs will "square up" the boxes and strengthen them.

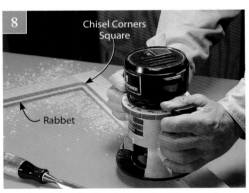

Rout the rabbets for the glass panels and square the corners with a chisel. Note: Have the glass cut ⅛ in. less than the rabbet width and height to insure a good fit.

Remove old tile, mantel and baseboard from the fireplace opening. The new tile is installed after the woodworking, staining and varnish are completed.

11. Join parts A and B to create the mantel face frame. Position the lower rail to accommodate the tile you've chosen. (We used 8 in. x 8-in. tiles. The actual size will vary.)

12. Assemble the mantel wall returns by screwing the cleats (K1 and K2) to the wall returns (L).

13. Make the built-up mantel top by gluing the bottoms and underlayment (T2 and T3) to the top (T1).

14. Glue ¼-in.-thick edge banding (S) to the outside edges. Be sure to miter the outside corners of the edge banding.

Building the Bookcases

1. Assemble bookcases (parts V through Z) using 2-in. wood screws (Photo 7). Then, drill holes for the adjustable shelves.

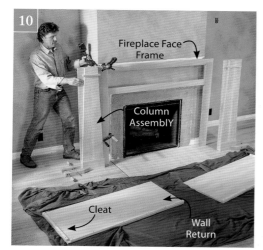

10

Fireplace Face Frame

Column Assembly

Cleat

Wall Return

Screw the column assemblies to the fireplace face frame. Prop the face-frame against the fireplace projection to make the job easier. Screw the plywood wall returns through the cleats to the column assembly from the inside (see Fig. E).

11

Wall Return

Cabinet Stile

Shims

Level each cabinet with shims. Then, scribe and plane the cabinet stile for a good fit against the wall return (Fig. C, Detail 1). Cover any gaps along the floor with trim molding (FF).

Oops!

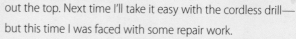

Errant Screw

The tops of these bookcases must be installed by screwing from underneath. Wouldn't you know it, the last screw to finish the job went too deep and came out the top. Next time I'll take it easy with the cordless drill— but this time I was faced with some repair work.

After backing out the offending screw, I carefully pushed the broken fibers back into place using a drop of glue to hold things together. Then I clamped a block of wood over the area to flatten the repair. I used some paper towels to absorb the squeeze-out under the clamping block. This kept the glue from spreading into the open grain of the oak where it would show up as a permanent mark after staining. Once the glue was dry I removed the clamp and lightly sanded the area. Now that nasty little hole is barely visible.

Paper Towel

2. Glue and clamp the face frames to each cabinet.

3. Biscuit or dowel the door frames together.

4. Rabbet the doors for the glass panels (Photo 8) and add the glass retainers.

5. Mount the doors to the bookcases using no-mortise hinges.

6. Make half-lap joints for the muntins on your tablesaw and assemble with a drop of glue.

7. Build-up and edge-band the bookcase tops in the same manner as the mantel top.

8. Cut and edge-band the shelves.

How to Make Bookshelves & Bookcases | **157**

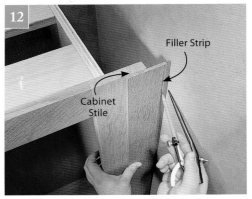

Hold the filler strip in place and scribe to fit the adjacent wall. Then, nail the strip onto the cabinet stile.

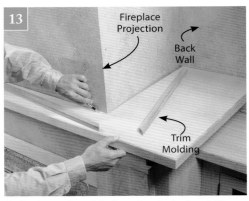

Scribe the top for a tight fit against the back wall. Then cover any gaps along the fireplace projection with trim molding (FF).

Secure the muntins to the glass with silicone caulk after the finish is dry.

Installation

1. Prepare the room for installation (Photo 9).

2. Assemble the mantel with 1¼-in. wood screws but leave the top off for now (Photo 10).

3. Screw three wall cleats (K3) along the back wall on each side of the fireplace to anchor the wall returns, as shown in Fig. E.

4. Push the entire assembly to the back wall and nail the face frame to the fireplace front wall and the wall returns to the wall cleats (Fig. E).

5. Level and fit the bookcases in the openings (Fig. C, Detail 1 and Photos 11 and 12). You may have to cut into the back of the cabinet if you need to make room for any wall receptacles. (See Safety Considerations, page 155 for more information.)

6. Once you're happy with the fit, screw the cabinets to the studs in the back wall with 3-in. wood screws.

7. Scribe the bookcase tops to fit. Then, screw them in place from underneath, using 1⅝-in. wood screws.

8. Scribe the mantel top to fit the back wall (Photo 13). Then nail the top down to the face frame, wall returns and wall cleats (Fig. C).

9. We finished the project with an oil stain and two coats of satin polyurethane for a deep and durable finish. After the finish dries completely (48 hours), install the tempered glass, hardware and muntins in the doors (Photo 14).

Cutting List

Part	Name	Qty.	Dimensions	Material
A	fireplace stiles	2	¾" x 4" x 50½"	oak
B	fireplace rails	2	¾" x 3" x 54"	oak
C	column backer stiles	4	¾" x 4" x 50½"	oak
D	column backer rails	8	¾" x 4" x 3½"	oak
E1	cabinet stiles	2	¾" x 3" x 44½"	oak
E2	cabinet stiles	2	¾" x 4" x 44½"	oak
F1	cabinet upper rails	2	¾" x 3" x 42"	oak
F2	cabinet lower rails	2	¾" x 5" x 42"	oak
G	upper door rails	4	¾" x 2¼" x 16⁷⁄₁₆"	oak
H	door stiles	8	¾" x 2¼" x 36⁷⁄₁₆"	oak
J	lower door rails	4	¾" x 3" x 16⁷⁄₁₆"	oak
K1	cleats	2	¾" x ¾" x 50½"	pine
K2	cleats	2	¾" x ¾" x 21¼"	pine
K3	wall cleats	6	¾" x 3½" x 10"	pine
L	wall returns	2	¾" x 22¾" x 50½"	oak plywood
M	taper-cut plywood	2	¾" x 9½" x 45½"	plywood
N1	column sides	4	¾" x 1¼" x 48"	oak
N2	column faces	2	¼" x 11" x 46½"	oak; trim to fit
P	column astragals	2	¾" x 2¼" x 7⅞"	oak
Q	column base fronts	2	¾" x 5" x 11"	oak
R	column base sides	4	¾" x 5" x 1¾"	oak
S	top edge banding	22 ft.	¼" x 1½"	oak
T1	mantel top	1	¾" x 26¾" x 88½"	oak plywood
T2	mantel underlayment front	1	¾" x 4" x 88½"	oak plywood
T3	mantel underlayment sides	2	¾" x 4" x 26¾"	oak plywood
U1	cabinet tops	2	¾" x 15¼" x 52"	oak plywood
U2	cabinet top underlayment	4	¾" x 4" x 52"	oak plywood
V	cabinet sides	4	¾" x 12" x 44½"	oak plywood
W	cabinet bottoms	2	¾" x 12" x 43"	oak plywood
X	partitions	2	¾" x 11¾" x 38¾"	oak plywood
Y	cabinet top strips	4	¾" x 4" x 43"	oak plywood
Z	cabinet backs	2	¾" x 44½" x 40½"	oak plywood
AA	unfaced shelves	8	¾" x 11⅝" x 21"	oak plywood
BB	shelf and partition facing	30 ft.	¼" x ¾"	
CC	filler strips	2	⅜" x 3" x 44½"	oak
DD	horizontal muntins	4	⅜" x ¾" x 16⁷⁄₁₆"	oak
EE	vertical muntins	8	⅜" x ¾" x 8"	oak
FF	trim	20 ft.	½" X ¾"	

by RANDY JOHNSON

Grand Bookcase

RICH WALNUT, ELEGANT DETAILS AND SECRET STORAGE IN A STRAIGHTFORWARD DESIGN

Sometimes a new piece of furniture conjures up images from a distant time and place. This bookcase, I imagine, would fit right into an early 20th-century lawyer's office, filled with leather-bound volumes and smelling of cigars. Rich walnut and generous moldings give it a luxurious feel, and hidden compartments are perfect for top-secret documents. The glass doors are as practical today for keeping dust off your books as they were 100 years ago. I've designed this bookcase for a thoroughly modern cabinetmaker, however. Its plywood cases are built with biscuits, the drawers use full-extension ball-bearing slides and the lipped doors are hung with easy-to-install wraparound hinges. To make this large project more manageable, I built it in sections: a drawer unit below, three separate bookcase units above and a crown molding unit on top. The modular design also makes it easy to move it around your shop and into your house.

A big project like this does require a bit of experience. You'll need to know

The modular design of this cabinet makes it easy to build and move.

Secret storage below the drawers provides a hiding place for valuables.

Lipped doors are easy to fit and hang and will even hide gaps caused by the doors being slightly warped or out of square.

how to use a biscuit joiner, be well-versed in using a router and router table and know how to install drawer slides. The only advanced technique you may need to know is how to make and install the custom crown molding. If you make the bookcase in oak or birch, you could buy commercial crown molding, but if you choose walnut or cherry, you'll probably want to make the molding yourself.

Start with the Drawer Base

1. Assemble the drawer base with biscuits, screws and glue. (Fig. A, Fig. D). The bottom and subtop (A1) are identical. Set the inner divider panels (A2) flush with the back edge of the subtop and bottom, leaving a ¼-in. space at the front. This space provides some clearance behind the drawer fronts. The side divider panels (A3) are set flush at the front and back of the subtop and bottom. After these parts are assembled, glue and clamp the fillers (A4) into place and add the spacer blocks (A5) to the front bottom edges of the vertical dividers (A2).

2. Add the walnut end panels (A6) to the drawer base (Photo 1). The end panels should extend ¼ in. behind the base bottom and subtop. This creates a lip for the back (A25) to fit into.

3. Join the wide bottom rail (A7) to the two side stiles (A8) with biscuits and attach this three-sided assembly to the plywood drawer base. Next, glue the narrow top rail (A9) directly to the front top edge of the drawer base between the side stiles (A8). Don't worry if the joint between these parts isn't perfect; a molding will cover it.

4. Attach the angled corner boards (A10) with cauls and clamps (Photo 2; Fig. H). I used my jointer to create the beveled edges

on these corner boards, but a fine-tooth blade in your tablesaw or a chamfering bit in a router table will also work. Using the dimensions from the Cutting List, page 170–171, will create corner boards that are slightly wider than needed so they will have a small overhang on each side when installed. The overhang makes fitting easier and is easily sanded off after the glue dries. Starting oversize is better than being undersize, which would expose the core of the plywood end panels (A6).

5. Add the base top (A11) to the drawer base. Leave it slightly oversize at the front and the ends and flush-trim it to match the base below (Photo 3). The back edge of the top should be flush with the back edges of the end panels (A6).

6. Use a roman ogee router bit in your router table to create the edge molding (A12, A13, A14) and the baseboard molding (A15, A16, A17) (Fig. K (page 168) for details on these moldings).

7. Attach the edge molding and baseboard molding with glue and a few brad nails. The miters on the baseboard use biscuits for alignment on the wide mitered joints. Note that the baseboard overhangs the bottom edge of the drawer base by ¾ in.

8. Screw the feet (A18) to the bottom of the drawer base.

9. Next, build the drawer boxes (A19, A20, A21). I built the drawers out of birch plywood and joined them with biscuits. This is simple and fast, but you can use any method you choose. The drawer

Both the lower drawer unit and the upper bookcase units have hollow ends. They act as torsion boxes, strengthening the units.

Gluing the angled corners can be tricky, but it's easy with a pair of plywood cauls. They hook around the front stile to prevent slipping and apply pressure to the corner's face.

Trim the base top of the drawer unit even with the case. A perfect fit is important, and it's much easier to achieve with a flush-trim router bit than by measuring and sawing.

Temporarily attach the drawer front with a few dabs of hot-melt glue. Open the drawer and drive in the screws that will permanently hold the front. When you're ready for finishing, remove the front and scrape off the hot glue.

bottoms (A21) fit in a quarter inch deep dado. Install the drawers on full-extension drawer slides.

10. Make the raised-panel drawer fronts (A22, A23, A24). I routed the raised panel so it stands proud of the drawer frame for a bolder look (Fig. J).

11. Screw the drawer front to the drawer boxes (Photo 4).

12. Screw on the back panel (A25).

Build the Three Bookcase Cabinets

13. Cut the plywood tops, bottoms, sides and fillers (B1 through B5) for the three bookcase units and assemble them with biscuits, glue and screws (Fig. B). Screw on the backs (B6, B7).

14. Add the outer side panels (B8) to the two outer cases.

15. Assemble face-frame parts (B9, B10, B11) with dowels or biscuits. Make sure the frames are square.

PROJECT REQUIREMENTS AT A GLANCE

Materials:
- Four sheets of ¾-in. walnut plywood
- Two sheets of ¾-in. birch plywood
- One sheet of ¼-in. birch plywood
- Two sheets of ¼-in. walnut plywood
- Birch edge banding
- 30 bd. ft. of 4/4 walnut
- 15 bd. ft. of 5/4 walnut

Cost:
- Materials and hardware, approximately $1,000

Hardware:
- 9⅜-in. lipped self-closing hinges
- Three pairs of 14-in. full-extension drawer slides
- Three panels of double-strength tempered glass for doors
- Four coupler bolts
- 42 glass retainer clips
- 48 shelf pegs
- 300 shelf peg hole grommets
- Three drawer pulls
- Three door pulls

Tools:
- Tablesaw
- Router bits
- Router table
- Planer
- Jointer
- Bandsaw
- Drill
- Biscuit joiner
- Miter saw
- Router
- Clamps
- Miscellaneous layout and hand tools

Figure A: Drawer Base Section Exploded View

This bookcase is built in easy-to-manage sections: a drawer unit below, three separate bookcase units above that and crown molding to top it off.

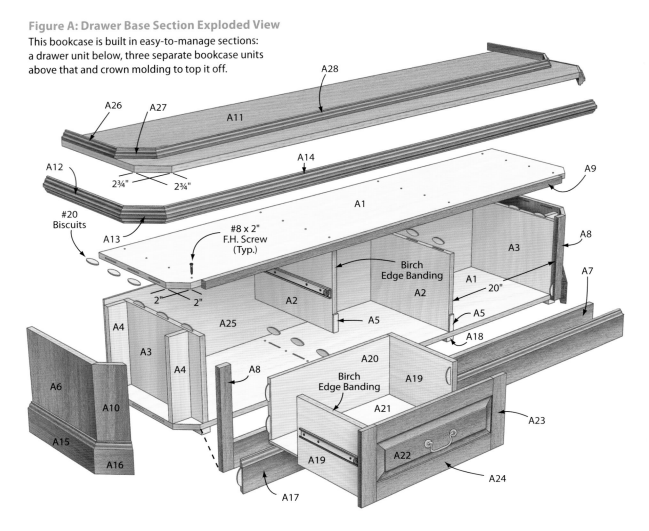

**Figure B:
Bookcase Section
Exploded View**

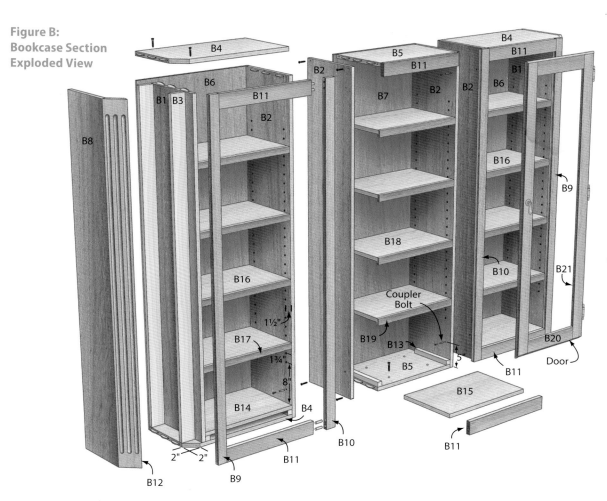

16. Glue the face frames to the two outer cases.

17. Attach the bottom and top rails (B11) to the center case (Photo 5). The center case is ⅛-in. narrower than the space it fills. This ensures that the ends of the rails (B11) will pull up tight to the stiles (B10) on the side cases.

18. Rout the flutes in the angled corner boards (B12, Fig. F; Photo 6) with a core box bit in your router table. Marks on the fence represent the start and end points of the flutes. Carefully lower the board onto

the core box bit to start the flute and tip the board up off the bit when it reaches the second mark. The only tricky thing about this fluting is that walnut tends to burn easily. Three precautions help you avoid burn: Use a new or freshly sharpened bit. Make the cut in several passes, with the final pass the lightest. Keep the work moving, because stopping creates extra friction, which can lead to burning.

19. Attach the fluted corner boards to the bookcases with the same clamping cauls that you used on the drawer base (Photo 2).

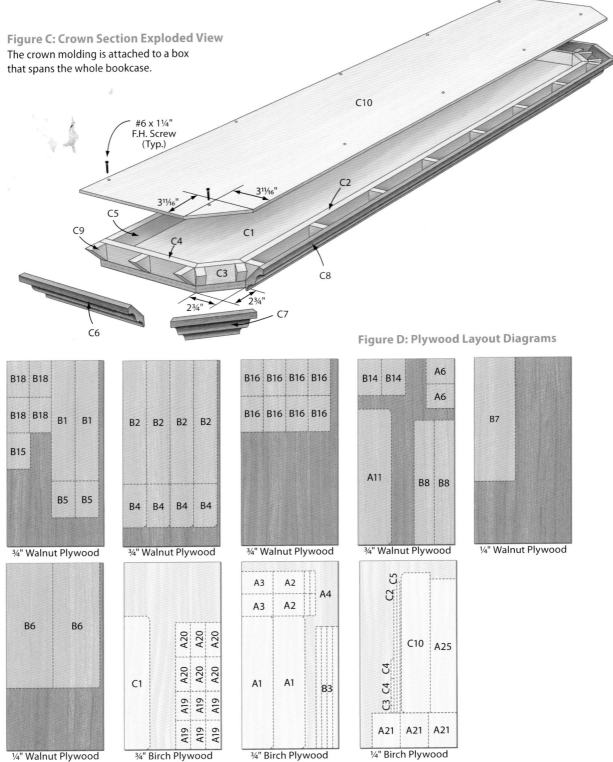

Figure C: Crown Section Exploded View
The crown molding is attached to a box that spans the whole bookcase.

C10

#6 x 1¼"
F.H. Screw
(Typ.)

3¹¹⁄₁₆"

3¹¹⁄₁₆"

C2

C5

C9

C4

C1

C3

C8

2¾"

2¾"

C6

C7

Figure D: Plywood Layout Diagrams

B18 B18

B18 B18 B1 B1

B15

B5 B5

¾" Walnut Plywood

B2 B2 B2 B2

B4 B4 B4 B4

¾" Walnut Plywood

B16 B16 B16 B16

B16 B16 B16 B16

¾" Walnut Plywood

B14 B14 A6

A6

A11 B8 B8

¾" Walnut Plywood

B7

¼" Walnut Plywood

B6 B6

¼" Walnut Plywood

C1

A20 A20 A20

A20 A20 A20

A19 A19 A19

A19 A19 A19

¾" Birch Plywood

A3 A2 A4

A3 A2

A1 A1 B3

¾" Birch Plywood

C2 C5

C3 C4 C4 C10 A25

C3 C4

A21 A21 A21

¼" Birch Plywood

The bookcase section is composed of three independent boxes, which make assembly a lot easier than handling one larger cabinet. The center unit, shown here, has bare plywood edges that will be covered by the side units' stiles.

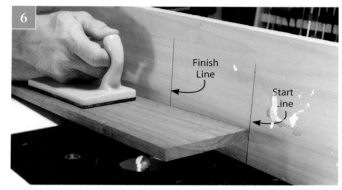

Flute the corner boards for the bookcases with a core box bit on your router table, tipping the board onto the router bit at the beginning and up at the end. Start and stop marks on the router fence provide the starting and stopping points of the flute.

Join the three bookcases with coupler bolts. Use a clamp to hold the cases together and double-check that the face-frame rails and stile line up flush at the top and bottom of the cases.

Assemble the doors. Check that they are flat by sighting down a pair of winding sticks. Add shims, if needed, under the clamps until the top edges of the winding sticks align with each other. After the doors are out of the clamps, to avoid warping, make sure to store them flat until you install them.

20. Stand the three cases on the drawer base.

21. Clamp the bookcases together, making sure the rails on the center bookcase line up flush with the face-frame stiles on the side bookcases. With everything aligned, drill the holes for the coupler bolts and install them (Photo 7).

22. Next, make sure the back of the bookcases and the back edge of the drawer base are lined up, with the bookcases centered left and right on the drawer base. With everything lined up, screw the bookcases to the drawer base using four 2-in. screws through the bottom of each bookcase section.

23. Add the shoe molding (A26, A27, A28, Fig. K) around the bottom of the bookcase units. Glue and brad-nail this molding to the top (A11) of the base, not to the bookcases.

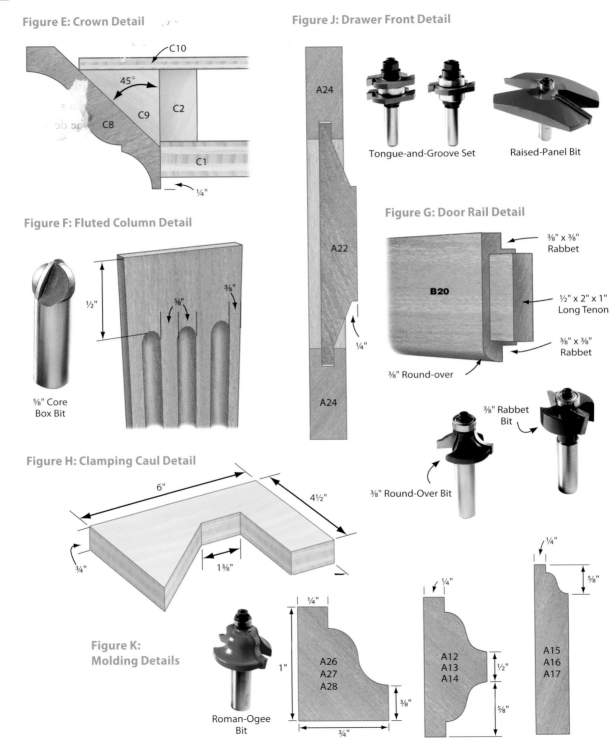

Figure E: Crown Detail

C10

45°

C2

C9

C8

C1

¼"

Figure F: Fluted Column Detail

½"

⁵⁄₈"

⅜"

⅝" Core
Box Bit

Figure J: Drawer Front Detail

A24

A22

¼"

A24

Tongue-and-Groove Set

Raised-Panel Bit

Figure G: Door Rail Detail

B20

⅜" x ⅜"
Rabbet

½" x 2" x 1"
Long Tenon

⅜" x ⅜"
Rabbet

⅜" Round-over

⅜" Rabbet
Bit

⅜" Round-Over Bit

Figure H: Clamping Caul Detail

6"

4½"

¾"

1⅜"

**Figure K:
Molding Details**

Roman-Ogee
Bit

¼"

1"

A26
A27
A28

⅜"

¾"

¼"

A12
A13
A14

½"

⅝"

¼"

⅝"

A15
A16
A17

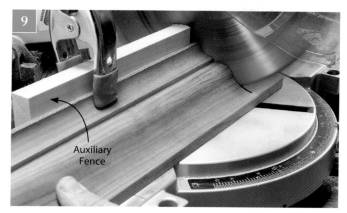

Cut the crown molding. Nesting the molding against the table and a tall auxiliary fence simplifies mitering, because it doesn't require a compound miter setup.

Attach the crown molding to the mounting board with a brad nailer. Use a spacer to create a lip on the bottom side. This lip will overhang the top edge of the bookcase units and hide the joint.

24. Screw the bottom spacers (B13) to the bottom of the bookcase and drop in the bottom shelves (B14, B15). The bottom spacers are shorter than the depth of the shelf space so you can push down on the back of the bottom shelves and tip up their front edges for removal. This even creates a little secret storage space.

25. Use a template and a self-centering bit to drill the holes for the shelf pegs and hole grommets.

26. Cut the shelves and glue on the edge banding (B16 through B19).

27. Make the doors (B20, B21). Mortise-and-tenon joinery provides strength and helps the doors glue up flat, but you should still use winding sticks to check the doors for flatness (Photo 8).

28. Use a round-over router bit to shape the outside corner of the door and a rabbeting bit to create the lip and the rabbet for the glass (Fig. G).

29. Hang the doors with ⅜-in. lipped hinges.

30. Measure the opening for the glass and allow ¹⁄₁₆-in. clearance all around. Install the glass using glass clips.

Add the Crown

You're not going to find walnut crown molding at your local home center or lumberyard, and buying such a small quantity from a custom molding shop is likely to be an expensive option. So here's a chance to get creative with your tablesaw. Another method for making it yourself is with a molding machine, such as the Woodmaster.

31. Start building the crown section (Fig C) by cutting the mounting board (C1) slightly oversize on the front and ends, screwing it to the top of the bookcases and flush-trimming the front and the ends the same way you did with the drawer base top (A11; Photo 3).

32. Remove the mounting board from the top of the bookcase and attach the edge boards (C2 through C5).

33. Next, cut the crown molding to size (Photo 9). A miter saw set at 22½ degrees is the perfect tool for this. If you use your tablesaw, you will need to set your blade to 15¾ degrees and your miter gauge to 73¾ degrees. Make sure to run some test pieces to check the settings.

34. Attach the crown molding (C6, C7, C8) to the mounting board with glue and brads (Photo 10, Fig. E).

35. Add glue blocks (C9) behind the crown molding for added strength (Photo 11).

36. Screw the crown assembly to the top of the bookcases and add the top panel (C10).

Add triangular glue blocks behind the crown molding for added strength. This crown assembly is screwed to the top of the bookcase.

37. Add the door and drawer pulls.

38. With the building completed, you can now disassemble the bookcase sections, do a final sanding and apply a stain and topcoat finish. I choose a dark stain and then applied a satin lacquer topcoat using an HVLP spray gun.

Cutting List

Overall Dimensions: 17½" D x 73¾" W x 81¼" H

Part	Name	Qty.	Material	Dimensions (TH x W x L)	Notes
Drawer base					
A1	Bottom and subtop	2	Birch plywood	¾" x 15¾" x 68½"	
A2	Inner divider panels	2	Birch plywood	¾" x 15½" x 11½"	Add iron-on edge banding to front edges.
A3	Side divider panels	2	Birch plywood	¾" x 15¾" x 11½"	
A4	Fillers	4	Birch plywood	¾" x 2¾" x 11½"	
A5	Spacers	2	Birch or walnut	¼" x ¾" x 2½"	
A6	End panels	2	Walnut plywood	¾" x 14" x 13"	
A7	Bottom rail	1	Walnut	¾" x 3¼" x 61½"	
A8	Stiles	2	Walnut	¾" x 1½" x 13"	
A9	Top rail	1	Walnut	¾" x 1" x 61½"	
A10	Corner boards	2	Walnut	½" x 4" x 13"	
A11	Base top	1	Walnut plywood	¾" x 16¾" x 70"	
A12	Waistband molding	2	Walnut	¾" x 1¾" x 14⁵⁄₁₆"	
A13	Waistband molding	2	Walnut	¾" x 1¾" x 4½"	
A14	Waistband molding	1	Walnut	¾" x 1¾" x 65⅛"	
A15	Baseboard	2	Walnut	¾" x 4" x 14⁵⁄₁₆"	
A16	Baseboard	2	Walnut	¾" x 4" x 4½"	
A17	Baseboard	1	Walnut	¾" x 4" x 65⅛"	

Part	Name	Qty.	Material	Dimensions (TH x W x L)	Notes
Drawer base *continued*					
A18	Feet	4	Birch or walnut	¾" x 1¼" x 15¾"	
A19	Drawer sides	6	Birch plywood	¾" x 7½" x 15"	Add iron on edge banding to top edges.
A20	Drawer fronts and backs	6	Birch plywood	¾" x 7½" x 17½"	
A21	Drawer bottoms	3	Birch plywood	¼" x 14" x 18"	
A22	Drawer panel	3	Walnut	¾" x 5¼" x 17⅛"	Finished drawer front should measure ¾" x 8⁹⁄₁₆" x 20⅜".
A23	Drawer stiles	6	Walnut	¾" x 2" x 8⁹⁄₁₆"	
A24	Drawer rails	6	Walnut	¾" x 2" x 17⅛"	
A25	Back panel	1	Birch plywood	¼" x 13" x 68½"	
A26	Shoe molding	2	Walnut	¾" x 1" x 10⁵⁄₁₆"	
A27	Shoe molding	2	Walnut	¾" x 1" x 4½"	
A28	Shoe molding	1	Walnut	¾" x 1" x 63⅝"	
Bookcase section					
B1	Sides	2	Walnut plywood	¾" x 11¾" x 62½"	
B2	Sides	4	Walnut plywood	¾" x 11¾" x 64"	
B3	Fillers	4	Birch plywood	¾" x 2¾" x 62½"	
B4	Tops and bottoms	4	Walnut plywood	¾" x 11¾" x 22½"	
B5	Tops and bottoms	2	Walnut plywood	¾" x 11¾" x 18⅞"	
B6	Backs	2	Walnut plywood	¼" x 23¼" x 64"	
B7	Backs	1	Walnut plywood	¼" x 20⅜" x 64"	
B8	Outer side panels	2	Walnut plywood	¾" x 10" x 64"	
B9	Stiles	2	Walnut	¾" x 1¾" x 64"	
B10	Stiles	2	Walnut	¾" x 2" x 64"	
B11	Rails	6	Walnut	¾" x 2½" x 18½"	
B12	Fluted corner boards	2	Walnut	½" x 4" x 64"	
B13	Spacers	6	Birch or walnut	1" x 1" x 9"	
B14	Bottom shelves	2	Walnut plywood	¾" x 11¹¹⁄₁₆" x 18⅞"	
B15	Bottom shelf	1	Walnut plywood	¾" x 11¹¹⁄₁₆" x 18¾"	
B16	Shelves	8	Walnut plywood	¾" x 11⅛" x 18⅞"	
B17	Edge banding	8	Walnut	⅜" x 1" x 18⅞"	
B18	Shelves	4	Walnut plywood	¾" x 11⅛" x 18¾"	
B19	Edge banding	4	Walnut	⅜" x 1" x 18¾"	
B20	Door rails	6	Walnut	⅞" x 3" x 15"	Includes 1"-long tenons.
B21	Door stile	6	Walnut	⅞" x 3" x 59½"	
Crown assembly					
C1	Mounting board	1	Birch plywood	¾" x 12¾" x 68½"	
C2	Front frame	1	Birch plywood	¾" x 1½" x 63"	
C3	Corner frames	2	Birch plywood	¾" x 1½" x 3⅞"	
C4	End frames	2	Birch plywood	¾" x 1½" x 10"	
C5	Back frame	1	Birch plywood	¾" x 1½" x 67"	
C6	Crown ends	2	Walnut	¾" x 4" x 11⅛"	
C7	Crown corners	2	Walnut	¾" x 4" x 6⅛"	
C8	Crown front	1	Walnut	¾" x 4" x 65¼"	
C9	Glue blocks	18	Birch plywood	¾" x 1⅝" x 1⅝"	
C10	Top panel	1	Birch plywood	¼" x 14⅜" x 71¾"	

RICHARD HELGESON

Sapele Display Cabinet

QUIET BEAUTY COMES FROM SUBTLE DETAILS

I designed this display cabinet to be a versatile, understated piece that will fit comfortably into a variety of interiors. The cabinet claims little more than a square foot of floor space, but will hold numerous objects on glass shelves. The back is quickly reversible (see photo at right), giving collectors different presentation options. Simple, rectilinear geometry frames and displays objects without competing for attention. The linear nature of ribbon stripe sapele veneers enhances the verticality of the piece. The built-up sides and top give the piece a sense of increased mass.

The cabinet is constructed using knock-down (KD) fittings—it will break down, pack flat and move or store easily. The structural core of the piece, a torsion box base with leveling feet, ensures that the cabinet reassembles consistently and will stand square and plumb on any floor surface.

Base Assembly

1. Cut the torsion box parts (A1-A3). Lay out the rib positions on the top and bottom panels and assemble with brads and glue (Photo 1). I use polyurethane glue here because it does not require much clamp pressure.

2. Cut the base panel (A4) and veneer with sapele (V1) on both sides (see "Veneer The Panels" (page 178)). Use scrap veneer for the underside where it won't be seen.

3. Locate the base panel so it overhangs the torsion box by ⅛-in. on all four sides and mark the outline on the shelf. Clip the heads from four small brads and set them point-up in predrilled holes inside the marked corners on the base panel. Align and press the torsion box onto the brads before gluing. This will locate the shelf during glue-up, and resist slippage as clamps or weight is applied.

4. Glue the bottom panel to the torsion box (Photo 2).

The display cabinet is built on and around a simple but strong torsion box. Use weight to clamp the top and bottom onto the web. Check for square before the glue sets.

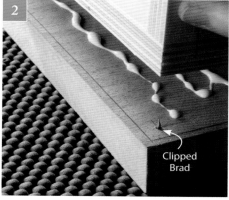

Glue the torsion box onto the base panel. Clip the heads off of brads and set them point up in holes in the panel. The brads keep the parts from shifting under clamp pressure.

5. Cut the baseboards (A5 and A6) and run a stopped groove on the top edge of the back baseboard to accept the back panel flange (Fig. A, Detail 1). Ease the outside edge of the groove slightly to make panel insertion easier.

6. Miter the baseboard to fit around the base panel.

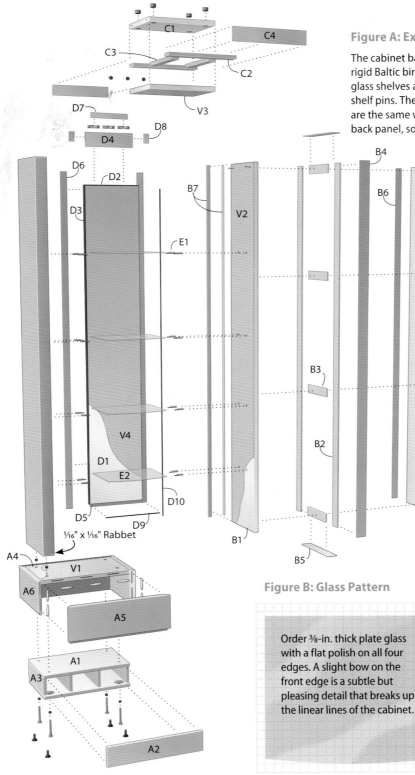

Figure A: Exploded View

The cabinet base is built around a flat and structurally rigid Baltic birch torsion box with leveling feet. The glass shelves are supported on shop-made aluminum shelf pins. The long pins suspend the shelves, which are the same width as the veneered portion of the back panel, so they appear to float in the cabinet.

Figure C: Shelf Placement

Drill ¼-in. holes for the shelf pins. You can drill a series of holes for adjustability if you like, but the cabinet looks best with just enough holes to support each shelf.

The spacing grows by an inch for each shelf from bottom to top. I think the impulse would be to space the shelves with the tallest opening at the bottom (like a chest of drawers). For this display cabinet, I like the tall opening at the top, because it puts the largest display area at eye level, and it balances the mass of the plinth-like base at the bottom.

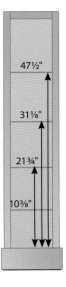

Figure B: Glass Pattern

Order ⅜-in. thick plate glass with a flat polish on all four edges. A slight bow on the front edge is a subtle but pleasing detail that breaks up the linear lines of the cabinet.

Cut biscuit slots in the base panel and the baseboard. The baseboard attaches to the shelf and floats free of the torsion box to allow for seasonal wood movement.

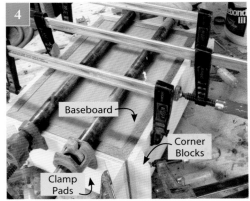

Clamp the baseboard to the base panel. Clamp pads made by gluing corner blocks to strips of plywood pull the miters tight. Use slow setting glues like Titebond III or Extend to ease the time pressures on the glue-up.

Assemble the side panels with glue and a brad nailer. Spacers add thickness to the sides and are positioned to support the panel when pressed for veneering.

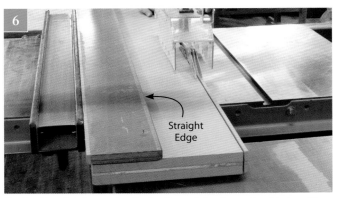

Rip the sides slightly oversize. Brad-nail a straightedge on the side to guide the first cut, then remove the straightedge and rip the opposite edge.

7. Cut biscuit slots to join the baseboard to the base panel (Photo 3) and to reinforce the baseboard miters. Position the slots so the baseboards are slightly higher than the top of the panel.

8. Glue and clamp the baseboard to the panel (Photo 4).

9. Clean up glue squeeze-out, and plane the baseboards flush with the base panel and with one another.

10. Cut a small rabbet along the bottom of the baseboard (Fig. A, Detail 1) to create a shadow line at the floor and lighten the visual mass of the base.

11. Locate and drill the holes for the threaded inserts in the base to accept the levelers (Fig. A, Detail 2). The threaded insert should be set under an outside rib.

12. Drill holes in the base for the confirmat screws (Fig. A, Detail 2).

Figure A: Detail 1 Back To Base

Note: Stop the groove 1⅞-in. from either end of the back baseboard (A6)

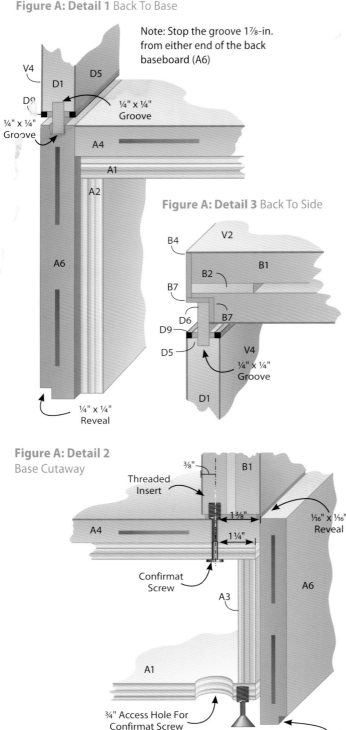

V4
D1
D5
D9
¼" x ¼" Groove
¼" x ¼" Groove
A4
A1
A2
A6
¼" x ¼" Reveal

Figure A: Detail 3 Back To Side

B4
V2
B2
B1
B7
D6
B7
D9
D5
V4
¼" x ¼" Groove
D1

Figure A: Detail 2
Base Cutaway

⅜"
Threaded Insert
B1
1⅜"
1¼"
A4
1/16" x 1/16" Reveal
Confirmat Screw
A3
A6
A1
¾" Access Hole For Confirmat Screw
Leveler
¼" x ¼" Reveal

Crosscut the ends of the side panel. Use a sled or miter gauge with a long fence.

Cut the seam where two veneers will join with a veneer saw. The veneer saw is designed to cut with several pull strokes. Lay the veneers face-to-face and hold them down with a straightedge as you cut.

Joint the two sawn veneer edges with a plane. Clamp the veneer face-to-face between two boards so it protrudes about ⅛-in. Then make a few light passes with the plane.

Tape the two veneers together with veneer tape. Solid, non-perforated tape works well, as it can be stretched slightly when it is applied. This helps pull the two pieces together.

Apply glue on the substrate only and lay down the veneer. A small roller works well to spread the glue quickly and evenly.

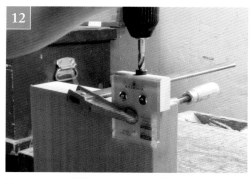

Use a commercial jig to locate and drill holes for the knockdown fittings between the top shelf and sides.

Clamp the back panel's ebony string detail with masking tape. The ebony comes in short lengths so butt-join the pieces end-to-end.

Side and Top Panel Construction

13. Rough cut panels (B1 and C1) about ½-in. oversize.

14. Glue-up the panels with spacers (B2, B3, C2 and C3) to create the thick sides and top (Photo 5). Pin the parts in place first with a brad nailer to keep them from skating under pressure. Use weight to clamp the panels.

15. Trim the panels square on the tablesaw (Photos 6 and 7).

16. Drill three shallow holes for the rare earth magnets across the back edge of the top panel and about 1½-in. in from either end (Fig. A.).

17. Apply the top and bottom edging (B5) to the side panels and the front and back edging (C4) to the top panel then plane flush.

18. Rip the side panels to final width, making a cut on each edge to leave the end caps perfectly flush with the sides.

19. Cut the top panel to final length in the same manner.

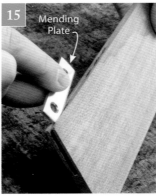

Use a thin kerf blade to cut a groove in the back's upper flange. Featherboards and push sticks are a must for this operation.

Mending plates are placed in the upper flange so magnets in the cabinet can hold the back in place. Add filler strips to encase the mending plates and fill the groove.

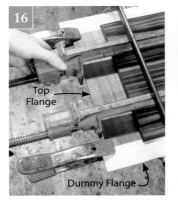

Glue the top and bottom flanges into the back first. Clamp dummy side flanges tight against the bottom of the side grooves to position the top and bottom flanges.

Rout flats on aluminum rod to create the shelf pins. Carbide bits can cut aluminum with ease. A ¼-in. deep V-groove in the jig holds the rod steady under the clamps.

20. Apply the front and back edge bands (B4, B6) on the side panels last to hide the end grain of the top and bottom edge bands. Applying the edge bands before veneering creates a seamless looking panel.

21. After the panel is veneered, cut the rabbet at the back inside edge of the sides panels (Fig. A, Detail 3). Add trim pieces (B7) to the rabbet.

Veneer The Panels

Note: If you can't find veneer wide enough to cover the panel, you'll have to seam it down the middle. If that is the case, try to order veneer that is slightly over half the finished width.

22. Cut the veneers (V2 and V3) to length and width with a straightedge and a veneer saw (Photo 8). For each seam, fold the faces against each other and cut them together. This creates a perfect 180-degree edge when the two leafs are unfolded.

23. Joint the sawn edges of the veneers with a plane (Photo 9).

24. Hold the veneer together with veneer tape (Photo 10). Tape every two inches perpendicular to the seam. Then add a long piece over the entire seam.

25. Apply glue in an even coat to the substrate and lay down the veneer (Photo 11). Specialized veneering glue, such as Titebond's Cold Press for Veneer, has a generous open time and is mixed with wood flour to minimize bleed through.

26. Prepare the panels for pressing by laying kraft paper over the veneer to absorb glue squeeze-out. Next add ¾-in. MDF platens under and over the panels to help distribute clamping pressure.

Note: In a vacuum press, the top platen should not overhang the substrate by more than ½-in. or it will lever up as the bag draws down and create areas of insufficient pressure.

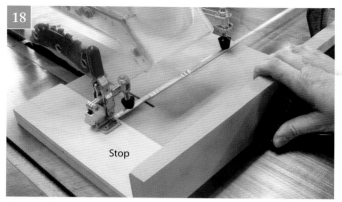

Crosscut the shelf pin blanks using a carbide blade and a slow feed rate. Secure the rod in a cut-off jig with two hold-down clamps. Place a stop at the desired length.

Smooth and polish the shelf pins with a mill file, sandpaper and steel wool.

27. Press the veneer onto the panels with a vacuum bag or by using platens with cross beams and clamps.

28. Trim the overhanging veneer with a router and a flush-cutting router bit.

29. Remove the veneer tape with a gentle sanding or dampen the tape and peel it off.

Note: Wait overnight before dampening to make sure the glue is fully cured.

30. Layout and drill the holes for the shelf pins (Fig. C), the threaded inserts (Fig. A, Detail 2) and the KD fittings at the top (Fig. A, Detail 4). Use a jig to locate and drill the KD fitting holes (Photo 12). Install the inserts and the KD fittings.

Back Panel Construction

31. Cut the MDF panel (D1) and apply the top edge band (D2) first. Cut and plane the edge band flush to the panel and apply the side edge bands (D3).

Figure A: Detail 5 Back/Top Cutaway

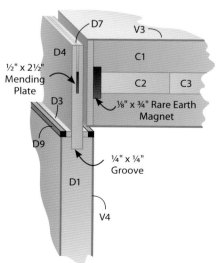

Figure A: Detail 4 Top KD Fitting

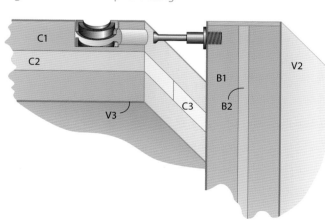

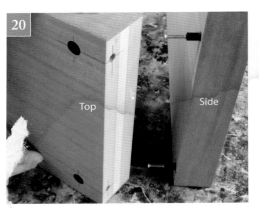

To assemble the cabinet, start by attaching the two sides to the top.

Thread a confirmat screw through the torsion box holes to attach the base to the sides. It helps to magnetize the wrench by rubbing it with a rare earth magnet first.

32. Seam and press veneer (D6) and trim flush.

33. Cut a ⅛-in. x ⅛-in. rabbet around the perimeter on both sides of the back. Glue the top and bottom ebony stringing (D9) on oversize (Photo 13). Do one side at a time, then plane flush. Apply the side stringing (D10) last.

34. Cut a groove centered on all four edges of the back panel (Fig. A, Detail 5) to accept the back flanges.

35. The top flange (D4) on the back has metal mending plates buried inside for the rare earth magnets to grab onto. Use a thin kerf blade on the tablesaw to cut a groove along the top edge of the flange (Photo 14).

36. Insert the mending plates and glue in filler strips (D7 and D8) to hold the plates in place (Photo 15).

37. Glue flanges (D4–D6) into the groove on the back panel. Glue the top and bottom flanges in first (Photo 16). Glue on the side flanges last.

Shelf Pins

38. To make the shelf pins, create a small flat on a length of ¼-in. aluminum rod with a carbide-tipped straight bit (Photo 17).

39. Cut the shelf pins to length (Photo 18).

40. File or sand the machined edges smooth (Photo 19).

Finish Up

41. Sand to 220-grit and finish the cabinet with oil, shellac, varnish or lacquer.

42. Attach the top shelf to the sides (Photo 20).

43. Attach the base to the sides with the confirmat screws (Photo 21).

44. Stand the cabinet up and adjust the feet to plumb the cabinet. Insert the pins and shelves, and you're finished.

Cutting List

Overall Dimensions: 70" H x 17" L x 10¾" D

Part	Name	Qty.	Dimensions (Th x W x L)	Material
A1	Torsion Box Top/Bottom	2	½" x 9" x 14¼"	½" Baltic Birch
A2	Torsion Box – Front/Back	2	½" x 3½" x 14¼"	½" Baltic Birch
A3	Torsion Box Sides/Ribs	4	½" x 3½" x 8"	½" Baltic Birch
A4	Base Panel	1	¾" x 9¼" x 14½" *	MDF
A5	Baseboard Front/Back	2	¾" x 6" x 16"	Solid Sapele
A6	Baseboard Sides	2	¾" x 6" x 10¾"	Solid Sapele
B1	Side Panels	4	¾" x 9¾" x 63¾" *	MDF
B2	Spacers – Long	4	¼" x 1½" x 63¾"	Poplar
B3	Spacers – Short	8	¼" x 1½" x 6¾"	Poplar
B4	Edge banding – Front	2	⅛" x 1¾" x 64"	Solid Sapele
B5	Edge banding – Top/Bottom	4	⅛" x 1¾" x 9¾"	Solid Sapele
B6	Edge banding – Back	2	⅛" x 1⅛" x 64"	Solid Sapele
B7	Edge banding – Rabbet	4	⅛" x ⅝" x 64"	Solid Sapele
Top Panel				
C1	Top Panel	2	¾" x 9¼" x 11" *	MDF
C2	Spacers-Long	2	½" x 1½" x 11"	Poplar
C3	Spacers-Short	2	½" x 1½" x 6¼"	Poplar
C4	Edge banding	4	⅛" x 2" x 11"	Solid Sapele
Back Panel				
D1	Back Panel	1	¾" x 9¾" x 60¾"	MDF
D2	Edge band – Top/Bottom	2	⅛" x ¾" x 9¾"	Solid Sapele
D3	Edge band – Sides	2	⅛" x ¾" x 61"	Solid Sapele
D4	Flange - Top	1	¼" x 2⅝" x 9½"	Solid Sapele
D5	Flange – Bottom	1	¼" x 1" x 9½"	Solid Sapele
D6	Flange – Side	2	¼" x 1⅜" x 64⅜"	Solid Sapele
D7	Fill Strip	1	³⁄₃₂" x ⅝" x 7½"	Solid Sapele
D8	Fill Strip Ends	2	³⁄₃₂" x 1⅛" x 1"	Solid Sapele
D9	Ebony Stringing – Top/Bottom	2	⅛" x ⅛" x 9¾"	Gabon Ebony
D10	Ebony Stringing – Sides	2	⅛" x ⅛" x 61"	Gabon Ebony
Veneer				
V1	Base Panel	2	9¼" x 14½" *	Sapele
V2	Side Panels	4	10" x 64" *	Sapele
V3	Top Panel	2	9½" x11" *	Sapele
V4	Back Panel	2	10" x 61" *	Bird's Eye Maple & Macassar Ebony
Miscellaneous				
E1	Shelf Pins	20	¼" x 1¾"	¼" Aluminum Rod
E2	Glass Shelves	5	⅜" x 8¾" x 10"	Plate Glass

* Cut oversize to allow for trimming

Index

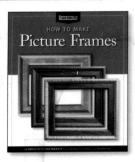
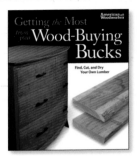
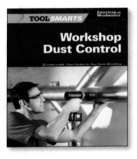

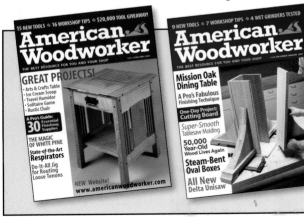